VISIONARY WOMEN

✦

THE TRIAL OF JOAN OF ARC

VISIONARY WOMEN

Also in this series:

THE MARTYRDOM OF PERPETUA
Sara Maitland

FLORENCE NIGHTINGALE:
LETTERS AND REFLECTIONS
Rosemary Hartill

Other titles in preparation

VISIONARY WOMEN ·

Series editor: Monica Furlong

THE TRIAL OF
JOAN OF ARC

with an introduction by

MARINA WARNER

ARTHUR JAMES

EVESHAM

First published in Great Britain in 1996 by

ARTHUR JAMES LTD
4 Broadway Road
Evesham
Worcestershire WR11 6BH

Introduction © Marina Warner 1996

Marina Warner asserts the moral right
to be identified as the author of the introduction to this work.

Text ©: see Acknowledgements

ISBN 0 85305 354 5

Typeset in Monotype Sabon by
Strathmore Publishing Services, London N7

Printed and bound in Great Britain by
Guernsey Press Ltd, Guernsey, C.I.

Contents

Series Foreword

Women, in our view, have always had interesting and valuable things to say about religious meaning, and about the life of the spirit, often with a different emphasis and accent from men writing and speaking about the same thing. It is not, probably, that women are so very unlike men. It is more that, historically, their life experience has been so different that, as you might expect, they saw events and ideas through a very different glass.

In the case of Christianity it is very difficult to know what they *did* see and feel. For the first eleven centuries of the Christian church they were almost completely silent, so far as writing and public speaking were concerned, forced to be so partly by lack of education, partly by those deadly chapters in the Epistles that commanded women to be 'silent in the churches', a prohibition that extended beyond the church in a framework that set up rigid conventions, confining women within home or convent. Very, very occasionally a woman's voice breaks through – as Perpetua tells us of the horror of her imprisonment before her martyrdom (third century), or the nun Egeria tells us of her travels (fourth century). It was only from the twelfth century onwards that voices of Christian women began, very tentatively, to emerge, or at least this was the time when women's writings began to be preserved so that they have come down to us.

Nor were other religions so very different. In widely

different cultures and religions – Judaism, Buddhism, Hinduism, Islam – it was assumed, as it was in Christianity, that caring for their husbands and bearing children somehow removed women from making any other sense of their lives or of the world about them. Of course women tried to do it – how can any human being not? – but their views were not sought or recorded.

As a Christian I cannot speak for other religions (though I hope others will speak for some of them in the course of the series), but I observe that everywhere women seem less and less willing to be silent and passive participants. Within Christianity now, there is a healthy and growing remorse for all that was lost when women's voices were silenced.

This series of books attempts to salvage some of the texts (often very little known even by feminists) which remind us what it sounded like when women first began to make their voices heard, and what they said as they described the experiences which shaped their thinking. It also uses material by later women who, one way or another, broke new ground in their actions, their ideas and their self-expression. Some of these are well known, but have often been presented to us in oddly distorted ways, which suggests that it is time for some reassessments.

It is not our intention to use these texts wholly uncritically – that would be to patronize the writers – but rather to use them to develop our own thinking. The early material, in particular, often needs effort, as it invites us to make use of ideas, and a view of religion, extraordinarily different from our own.

Our hope is that readers will want to make a small

collection or library of these precious texts – a reparation to the forgotten women, but also, we believe, a fruitful source of inspiration and ideas for ourselves, the fortunate heirs of their courage and determination.

MONICA FURLONG

Acknowledgements

Marina Warner thanks all her colleagues at Erasmus University, Rotterdam, where she was Tinbergen Professor in 1991, and especially Dr Jan van Herwaarden, who organised the Joan of Arc symposium at which she presented a version of the Introduction to this volume.

Editor and publisher would like to thank the Folio Society, London, for permission to use extracts from the translation by W. S. Scott of the Orléans Manuscript, published by the Society in 1956.

Introduction

Joan of Arc: a gender myth

Joan of Arc is the only saint of the church who was burned by the same church as a heretic, an idolater, and an apostate. She was burned in 1431 in the marketplace at Rouen after a prolonged and elaborate Inquisition trial which was attended by most of the learned prelates and lawyers in the north of France at that time. [1*] Sometimes more than seventy men attended a single session to listen to the cross-questioning of an illiterate peasant from Lorraine who had barely learned to write her name. Yet, by the special combination of her character and her circumstances, Joan of Arc has come to occupy as crucial a place in the history of gender definition as she did in the political outcome of the Hundred Years War.

Her trial is a very rare testimony to a young woman's life and thinking, and now I want to look at it with regard to changing ideas about female deviation and witchcraft. For there are two aspects of her story which I think need modifying since I wrote my book in 1981 and made the film for television in 1983. [2] First, our perception of witchcraft in the fifteenth century has been influenced by later witch trials, taking place in the sixteenth and seventeenth centuries, so that when we look at the question of

---

* Numbers in square brackets, e.g. [4], refer to the Notes which begin on p. 165.

witchcraft as raised by Joan of Arc's trial we see it filtered through a glass of fantasies that arose a hundred years after her death, and this is clearly an error. [3] Second, I want to review how her masculinity, her boyishness, her cross-dressing has come to be intertwined with our changing ideas about female virtue.

On Laetare Sunday, which falls in the middle of Lent on the fourth Sunday after Shrove Tuesday – that is, in the spring – the young people of the village of Domrémy, the village where Joan of Arc was born, took a picnic to a large tree, and ate and drank there together, singing and dancing and making garlands to hang on the branches. These swept down to the ground and made, according to a later traveller, a kind of natural chamber within [4]. Joan of Arc said at her trial that she went there with the other young women to bring back 'le beau mai' (beautiful mayblossom) – this is a springtime flower associated with the Virgin Mary, and before her, with the mother goddesses of pre-Christian Europe. [5] Robert Graves, for instance, in *The White Goddess*, dwells on the symbolism of may blossom, and its erotic connections: its scent is not fragrant like roses, but musky, almost animal. For this reason, he says, it has been associated with female powers of generation. [6]

The tree where they made their picnic was known as '*l'arbre des fées*' ('the fairies' tree'). Fairies then did not have the connotations they have now, with the wonder-workers of fairytales, with the 'little people', or the 'wee folk' as they are known in Celtic tradition and appear in Shakespeare.' [7] The mischievous elves and goblins, pixies and sprites of familiar stories today, who live in the grass under toadstools, or, like Ariel in *The Tempest,* in a cowslip's bell, belong to northern traditions of folklore, and do not populate the myths and legends of France before the seventeenth century. [8] In the fifteenth, in Joan of Arc's time, the fairies were *fatae,* fates – they descended from the classical three sisters who spun and cut the thread of life, the *Parcae.* [9] Their name, derived from the Latin for speech – from the verb *fari, fatum,* 'to speak', testifies to their oracular function – when they uttered, they determined a person's fate, seeing into the past and into the future. It is not be difficult to see the kinship between the grim sisters of classical mythology and the witches of medieval Christian folklore. [10]

The good and bad fairies of stories like 'The Sleeping Beauty' or 'Cinderella', which were written down in the late seventeenth century, crystallized tales which had been told orally for centuries before. [11] When Carabosse, in 'The Sleeping Beauty', lays the curse on the princess because she has not been invited to the christening, she recalls the behaviour of the goddess Eris (Strife), who alone among the immortals was not asked to the wedding of Peleus and Thetis. To avenge herself, she cursed her fellow divinities by throwing down the apple of discord at the feast. [12] The malevolence of fairies was common in fairytales – one of the group of French fairytale writers, Louise d'Auneuil, even celebrated the undoing of their powers in *La Tyrannie des fées détruite* (1702). By the nineteenth century, however, a clear distinction had emerged between on the one hand fairies, like Cinderella's godmother, who do good, wear butterfly wings, have stars on their wands and wear pink, and on the other hand witches, who do evil and are ugly and grotesque old women who also possess supernatural powers but use them mainly to do harm. [13] In the first decades of the fifteenth century, this manichaeism did not obtain, and certainly not in Domrémy: the fairies of the tree were considered ancient powers, with the potential of good or ill, possessed of visionary and oracular faculties. [14]

They were also female, without question, or surprise. The Sunday on which this local, rustic custom took place was also known in Domrémy, we learn from Joan of Arc's trial, as the '*dimanche des fontaines*'. The young people of the neighbourhood returned from the tree and on the way back, stopped to drink at a certain fountain known as 'the Frogs' spring' (later to be named 'the Gooseberry Bush fountain'). [15] There they made offerings, picked flowers, enjoyed themselves, and generally made merry. Again, the custom reflects ancient rites: the pagan spring festivals were also a time of rejoicing, and the holy character of wells, where wishes can be made, continues from the pre-Christian past into the present day. Wells are a place of meeting, of talk, too, and in folklore, the site where the heroine often meets a fairy, disguised as an old woman, who might ultimately reward her for her kindness. Many saints are still connected with wells of healing and prophecy and also now many people will have come across such a sanctuary in their travels. In Germany, the powerful Frau Holle, in the Grimms' famous story, lives at the bottom of a well, where she controls nature, the weather, and the fortunes of young girls. [16] The Grimms were writing in the early nineteenth century, but their fairytales record ancient oral material, and dig deep into the strata of old European mythology.

At the trial, Joan of Arc was repeatedly interrogated

about her activities on the Sunday of the Fountains by *l'arbre des fées*. She was forthright, honest, as she always was – we can hear her conviction of her own innocence of mischief in the fullness of her answer:

> there was a tree which was called the Ladies' tree; others called it the Fairies' tree, and near it there was a spring; and she had heard it said that persons suffering from fever drank of it; and she has seen them going to it to be cured. But she did not know whether they were cured or not. ... She had heard several old folk say ... that the fairies frequented it [the tree]; and she heard her godmother Jeanne ... say that she had seen them there. Whether this was true, she does not know. She said that she herself had never seen a fairy, as far as she knew, either at the tree or anywhere else.

Joan then went on to talk of a wood near Domrémy, called '*le bois chesnu*' – meaning either 'the oak wood' or 'the hoary wood' – and volunteered to the court that she had not heard there were fairies there either. But her brother had told her there was a rumour that she had received her message at the tree. At this session of the trial, she explicitly denies it. [17]

But on 1 March, the next session, she went back on her assertion, and said that she did not know if she had seen Saints Catherine and Margaret at the tree, but she had seen them at the fountain. [18] Tradition has disregarded the several inconsistencies in Joan's account, selecting as it sees fit; today, at her shrine in Domrémy, she is represented seeing her voices near the tree, in one section of the fresco cycle with which the nineteenth-century church is decorated, and in hagiographical materials, such as a photograph of a *tableau vivant* staged around 1900,

Saints Catherine, Margaret and Michael again appear to her under the broad shade of a large tree. [19]

In 1429, in Paris, a rival prophetess, Catherine de la Rochelle, had been questioned about Joan of Arc, and had told the tribunal that Joan was advised by two mentors she called the 'advisers of the fountain'. [20] Catherine de la Rochelle was also a visionary. In her case, a '*dame blanche*' or 'white lady', wearing a golden crown, appeared to her at night and gave her instructions about the Valois campaign in France. In the winter before she was captured, Joan invited Catherine to share her visions with her – and they spent a night waiting together for *la dame blanche* to appear. Joan fell asleep, and when she woke, Catherine told her that she had missed the lady. The next day, Joan slept so that she would be able to keep awake at night. But the white lady never appeared, though Catherine kept protesting that she would, soon. [21]

This trial of authenticity between Catherine and Joan over a supernatural adviser is exceptionally interesting. First, it reveals that Joan was willing to believe that Catherine's *dame blanche* was a possibly genuine visitation; this suggests that the Christian character of her own voices, their identity with angels and saints, did not seem to her a necessary condition of their existence. Catherine de la Rochelle's *dame blanche* in a golden crown seems a purely secular figure, concerned only with the battle plans and strategy.

Second, Joan of Arc clearly believed that others, beside the seer, were able to share in a vision: again, not a characteristically Christian approach to mystical phenomena, which are usually reserved for the seer alone, and invisible to others, as described in the lives of saints as famous as

Saint Francis of Assisi, or more recently, Saint Bernadette. But in Joan's case, many witnesses at Chinon, where the court was staying, said that they too had seen the vision of the crown which she described to Charles the Dauphin. Joan of Arc invoked this as a precedent herself at her trial, telling her interrogators that she would not have asked or expected to see Catherine's *dame blanche* unless she had not been told by so many people that they too had seen the divine signs that appeared to her. [22]

Third, Joan's visions, like Catherine de la Rochelle's, did not invoke the prime movers of the Christian scheme of salvation, like the Virgin Mary or Jesus. Indeed her voices' identities – Michael, Catherine and Margaret – were only established midway through the long trial, after intense interrogation. [23] Earlier, Joan had told one of her companions-at-arms, Comte Dunois, that she had seen Charlemagne and St Louis – appropriate visions in the midst of a political and military campaigns as for the French in those days both were Kings of France who fought as crusaders. Joan of Arc often spoke of the struggle against the English in crusading terms. [24]

Joan's belief in the possibility of sharing her visions with others and vice versa connects interestingly with an aspect of the ancient witchcraft: that witches were believed to gather together and conjure supernatural phenomena in a group. Female sorcery was perceived to be a communal activity, rather similar to work in the kitchen or the laundry or the hospice. There has been a recent revival of interest in Margaret Murray's theory, that the ancient religion centred on goddess worship and animal rites and sacrifices survived in Europe throughout the Christian period, with women as its votaries and ministers. [25] Her theory enjoyed great popularity, but has since been discredited as a fantasy by historians and anthropologists, like Norman Cohn. [26] The historian Carlo Ginzburg has now returned to it, and broadly endorsed Jung, in a new study called *Storia notturna*, which was translated into English as *Ecstasies*. [27] Ginzburg argues that previous writers on the subject of witchcraft become far too absorbed in the paranoia of the inquisitors and lose sight of the actual beliefs and interests of their victims; paying attention to what the accused say yields, he argues, a picture of folk religion persisting undiminished in the countryside all over Europe. Though not entirely persuasive, the book is definitely worth looking at. And it illuminates some of the Joan of Arc evidence. It shows that in the minds of the people trying Joan of Arc and in the practices in her village as well there may well have been strong vestiges of pre-Christian attitudes to supernatural phenomena.

The judges in Rouen in 1431 did not return to the subject of the fairies' tree in their condemnation of Joan of Arc – they did not insist on the connection between the voices who gave her her mission and the sacred tree of her village, whether or not it represented the survival of pagan cults. They abandoned this line of questioning, and concentrated on the appearance and messages of Joan's voices in particular, not the place where they had made themselves manifest. In general, the trial shifted from an attempt to identify Joan with witchcraft towards proving her a heretic; in this the judges were following ecclesiastical law as set out in the papal bull *Super illius specula*, of 1326–7, where it was stipulated that the church should proceed against practitioners of ritual magic as against heretics. It was not the purpose for which the demons were summoned that constituted the sin; rather the invocation itself in the first place revealed the apostasy of the magician or witch. [28] Consequently wisewoman magic, used for good ends, as in healing, incurred equal guilt as necromancy or alchemy or other maleficium.

The trial at Rouen made several attempts to prove that Joan had practised magic. But as with the accusation that she had joined in the dancing beneath the fairy tree, the charges failed to stick. Joan of Arc stubbornly refused to fit the prevailing idea of a sorceress, as we shall see. However, the trial's vagueness on this point greatly exercised the next generation in France, when Joan of Arc was cleared of the Rouen charges in the posthumous trial of rehabiliation in 1456, twenty-five years after she was burned at the stake. Several witnesses who had known her when she was living in Domrémy were questioned about her conduct as a child and later as a young woman; they were given a list of twelve topics. The ninth specifically focused on *l'arbre des fées*, and in response, many of them produced interesting circumstantial evidence about the villagers' beliefs. [29] One 80-year-old woman said that the fairies no longer came to the tree, on account of the people's sins – the Christian shift towards identifying the fairies with a moral economy rather than with simple animist powers registers strongly in this witness's testimony. [30] Another, a 50-year-old man, remembered that the pilgrimage to the tree took place on more than one feastday – and in the month of May as well, and that the young people made 'a man of May' there as well as bringing bread and wine and dancing. [31] The figure of a green man or other form of vegetal force is a very ancient symbol of the spring, and survives in folklore today, in many countries' carnival traditions. (In England, for instance, Jack-in-the-Green [32] was still paraded through the streets by chimney sweeps in London in the nineteenth century.) The evidence at the rehabilitation trial of 1456 emphasized the innocence of the country custom, and exonerated Joan from any sinister relationship with the woods or the spirits of past creeds dwelling therein.

This rehabilitation trial did however return persistently to the theme of *l'arbre des fées* because during the first half of the fifteenth century the practice of witchcraft, and fears of its effects, significantly increased and spread in France. During Joan's brief life, acute terror of witchcraft had begun to penetrate the most educated levels of secular society – earlier, I think one can say, in the fourteenth century, it was churchmen who principally suffered from such fears. [33] But when John the Fearless, Duke of Burgundy, was murdered in 1419, his right hand was cut off to prevent him continuing to practise in death the sorcery he had practised in life. Before him, his cousin, Louis of Orléans, had been assassinated – and the assassination justified, from the pulpit, by a sermon which declared that he was a magician, who deserved to die. [34] Two of Joan of Arc's companions-in-arms – the Duke of Alençon and the notorious 'Bluebeard', Gilles de Rais, were tried for sorcery, albeit the last above all for treason. Gilles de Rais was executed in 1440 and D'Alençon was proved guilty twice, in 1458 and in 1474; however, although condemned to death on the second occasion, he died in his bed in 1476. [35] Among the English, matters were not very different: in 1441 Eleanora Cobham, Duchess of Gloucester and sister-in-law of the very Duke of Bedford who was Regent of France and Joan of Arc's goaler at Rouen, was denounced for using witchcraft to depose or kill the boy king of England, Henry VI. Her associates were hanged and burned, but her life was spared; she was condemned instead to walk the streets of London in penitential dress, and was then exiled to the Isle of Man. [36] In Basel, between 1431 and 1438, the very time of Joan's death, Johannes Nider wrote one of the crucial documents of the later persecution of suspected witches, the *Formicarius*. Nider wrote that 'There are three things in nature which, if they transgress the limits of their conditions, whether by diminution or by excess, attain the highest pinnacles, whether of goodness or of evil. These are the tongue, the ecclesiastic and woman. All these are commonly best of all so long as they are guided by good spirit but worst of all if guided by evil spirit.' [37] The questions of women and possession, of women's speech and maleficium, were squarely raised in this cleric's meditation on the work of the devil in the world.

The witch trials of the early fifteenth century still do not yet present the familiar picture of witchcraft or witches: the prosecutors do not invoke devil-worship at sacrilegious masses, flying to gatherings of the Sabbath, the collective blasphemies of the witches' coven, the perverse eroticism and cannibalism which emerge in the charges of witch-hunters in the sixteenth and seventeenth centuries, and were depicted with such intensity and fascination by artists like Lucas Cranach the Elder, in his study of *Melancholy*, or Hans Baldung Grien in drawings of the 1510s and 20s, and by Jacob Cornelisz van Oostsanen, in his large painting of 1526, *Saul and the Witch of Endor*, in the Rijksmuseum at Amsterdam. [38]

The textbooks of the inquisitors, like the *Malleus Maleficarum,* where these fantasies appear, had not yet been compiled (it was published in 1486). But in Switzerland, the Vauderie, or persecution of the Waldensians, was under way by the last years of Joan's life, and some of the charges against these heretics antic-ipate the features of the early modern witchhunt: they were accused of night-flying, for instance, and inspected to uncover 'witch's marks', the supposed badge of devil-worshipper. [39]

It is interesting therefore to scrutinize the trial of Joan of Arc in the light of this increasing fear of witches among the learned, the nobility and the clergy. The judges returned again and again to several incidents in her career: the episode at Lagny, when a dead baby was brought out to her and revived at her touch, surviving long enough to be baptized. Dead babies are of course the staff of life to witches in folklore: but they do not get revived. The judges tried hard to pin responsibility for the baby's death on Joan, but failed. There were other prodi-gies reported that excited the judges' suspicions: butter-flies had fluttered around her banner at Château-Thierry, during the military campaign. Butterflies, like toads and lizards, symbolized dead souls, and were considered the familiars of witches. Joan had revealed she possessed a diviner's powers, when she foresaw in a dream the where-abouts of her miraculous sword and found it, as foretold, under the altar at the chapel St Catherine de Fierbois, when she located a lost cup belonging to one of her peti-tioners, and identified a bad priest who was living in sin with his housekeeper. She was accused of using a man-drake root as a charm. [40] Joan denied all this, except the discovery of her sword. The Englishmen and their Burgundian allies, putting her on trial, were not convinced of her innocence, for her reputation for magical powers had been established throughout the fighting, by her apparent invulnerability to wounds, by her knowledge of the outcome of the battles and her general prophetic faculty. The Duke of Bedford referred to her as 'a disciple and lyme of the feende called the Pucelle'. [41]

Joan herself knew the current beliefs about her: in July 1429, on her way to Reims to crown the Dauphin, she was met at the gate of the city of Troyes by a friar called Brother Richard, who sprinkled her with holy water to exorcise her, as the people feared that she was 'not a thing from God'. Joan called out to him, with her robust good humour, 'Approach boldly! I shall not fly away.' [42] She knew that witches – like fairies – could fly. At the end of the preparatory interrogation Joan was asked again about fairies, this time with the question whether she knew anything of those who consorted with them. 'She answered that she herself never did so, or knew anything about it, but she had heard it said that they went on Thursdays, but she does not believe in it and thinks it only sorcerie.' [43]

In the context of the growing European witchhunt and the prevailing fears of Joan's contemporaries, both on her side and on her enemies', it is surprising that in the final decree of the court she was not declared a witch. The verdict of the Inquisition prevaricated: 'Having weighed the aim, manner and matter of [Joan's] revelations, the quality of her person, and the place and other circumstances, they are either lies of the imagination, corrupt and pernicious, *or* the said apparitions and revelations are conjured up and proceed from malign and diabolical spirits Belial,

Satan, Behemoth.' [44] The alternative admits doubt – doubt that does not govern the outcome of trials which preceded hers. The judges at Rouen would have condemned Joan as a sorceress if they could; but they did not.

Two women had been burned, for instance, in 1390–91 in Paris: Margot de la Barre was charged with employing Marion la Droiturière to make her ex-lover impotent with his young wife. They were both tortured, and confessed that they had dealt with the devil and that he had given them a chaplet of herbs with magic powers. Another woman, Macete, was accused of asking Jehane de Brigue to make a certain man fall in love with her and marry her – the spell worked, but her husband beat her, so she then tried to make him ill using wax figures and toads. Both confessed under torture, and were eventually burned as witches. [45] The inquisitors threatened to put Joan of Arc to the question – to torture her, but in the end they refrained, for reasons that are not given. [46] And as a result, almost certainly, they did not achieve enough evidence of her intercourse with devils to declare unequivocally that she was a witch.

In the sixteenth century, she was nevertheless considered to have been a witch. Shakespeare's *Henry VI, Part One,* written at the start of the poet's career during a peak of the great witchhunt, was based on Burgundian and English chronicles of the Hundred Years' War, and the verdict of the trial had not modified popular opinion as to Joan's contact with the devil. Shakespeare's Joan conjures evil spirits and promises them further, gruesome sacrifice:

> O, hold me not with silence over-long!
> Where I was wont to feed you with my blood,
> I'll lop a member off and give it you. [47]

But the judges at Rouen could not be convinced, for several reasons. Above all, Joan's virginity proved her virtue; it contradicted all the known lewdness and sensuality of the devil's dames, the witches. [48] The depths of her heresy, however, showed in other aspects of her belief and behaviour. The trial concentrated on two in particular, and the sentences of condemnation returned to them again and again: the character of her visions, and her male attire.

Peter Brown has written about the context which allows such fears to take hold and flourish:

> This is when two systems of power are sensed to clash within the one society. On the one hand, there is articulate power, power defined and agreed upon by everyone (specially by its holders); authority vested in precise persons; admiration and success gained by recognised channels. Running counter to this there may be other forms of influence less easy to pin down – inarticulate power: the disturbing intangibles of social life, the imponderable advantages of certain groups, personal skills that succeed in a way that is unacceptable or difficult to understand. Where these two systems overlap, we may expect to find the sorcerer. [49]

Joan of Arc presents us with a case of inarticulate power investing itself with all the accoutrements and style of articulate power. She became in a sense more suspect because she did not appear to use sorcery to achieve her ends, and yet, being the person she was, a young female peasant, she should not have been able to occupy such a position of influence, or voice the ideas she had and reach a wide following. Nothing could be more conventional than Joan's stance during the years of her public mission

– except that she was the wrong person to embody those conventions: she was not a man of the church, who could legitimately claim to receive messages from God via his saints and angels, she was not a nobleman of the world, who could legitimately claim to fight as a knight for his suzerain. She transgressed against class, sex, social boundaries and feudal expectations: the transgression lent her charisma, and earned her immense influence for a while. [50] But the inappropriateness of her conduct made her position dangerous; it is the hardest thing for a social anomaly to become a regular and accepted member of the dominant group, of the centre of power. For Joan's enemies, her witchcraft lay not in the spells or charms or wonders she had accomplished, but in the phenomenon of articulate power itself exercised from a source that due order would require to remain inarticulate. [51]

The struggle to legitimize Joan's counterfeit masculinity and knightliness began in her own lifetime. After the raising of the siege of Orléans in 1429, the poet Christine de Pisan, breaking a long silence, greeted the rise of a saviour for France with her long poem *Le Ditié de la Pucelle*. [52] Christine invokes precedents for the warrior maid and her virtuous championship of the forces of good. She compares Joan to the biblical heroines Esther, Judith and Deborah, and then goes on to declare that Joan surpasses them in greatness, and indeed resembles no less a trinity of heroes than Hector, Joshua and Achilles. [53]

Joan loathed women-campfollowers and she is told to chase those girls using the flat of her sword, once so hard that she broke her sword. [54] Stories about Joan's chasing loose women became very popular as is proved by an illustration in a manuscript with the *Vigiles de*

Charles VII, a biography in verse, written by Martial d'Auvergne in 1484. The illustrator interpreted Joan's action in a different spirit – in one image, she resembles the spirit of Justice, avenging humanity against the sirens and temptresses who lead man into sin, just as in traditional medieval iconography, depicting the allegory of Everyman's weakness, the personified virtue of Justice is represented attacking the embodied vices who tempt him to sin. In a sixteenth-century tapestry in Hampton Court Palace, London, for instance, Mercy tries to restrain the anger of Justice. [55] Justice, the armed maiden of conventional personification, became one of the moulds into which Joan of Arc was poured in order to lessen the threatening character of her cross-dressing. Another exemplary prototype was Judith, the biblical heroine whom Christine de Pisan had invoked. In Martin Le Franc's poem of 1440, *Le Champion des Dames,* he compares Joan of Arc to Judith, who battled to deliver her people from tyranny. Le Franc was a Burgundian, but he defends Joan from the accusations of devil-inspired deviancy by saying that she needed to wear a short coat and breeches, just as a falcon needs to be freed from his jesses in order to fly free on the hunt. [56]

The viragoes of classical and biblical legend were not the only witnesses for the defence in the matter of Joan's transvestism. Joan was using male apparel to appear sexless, rather than male, to appear not-female, rather than female. She was not in disguise – everybody knew that she was Joan la Pucelle, the magic virgin. Female in body, but not in spirit – her dress signified her abjuration of the weakness of femininity, both physical and spiritual. Her predecessors in this denial of gender were the angels, who in representations of her time were highly androgynous in appearance. [57] This is especially true of St Michael, one of her voices, who together with the archangel Gabriel, was depicted on the banner she carried into battle. [58]

Yet at the same time, cross-dressing was forbidden – the Bible calls it an abomination, in Deuteronomy 22, and St Paul had expressly forbidden women to cut their hair. [59] The debate about the propriety of her clothes and her hair, 'cropped round in man's style', was fierce during Joan's early career – churchmen of great standing argued for and against her in this matter. [60] But the judges were absolutely clear that she contravened natural law and God's law when she refused to wear a woman's dress, and they would not allow her to go to mass and receive communion, which she craved, unless she agreed to change out of her breeches. She refused, then changed her mind, then refused again – it is possible that her woman's dress was deceitfully taken away, preventing her from doing as she had promised. [61] On the other hand, she also clings verbally with remarkable intensity to her male apparel. The men's clothes she wore became the burden of no less than five of the seventy articles in the charges of condemnation at the end of the trial. One of them reads as follows:

> The said Jean put off and entirely abandoned women's clothes, with her hair cropped short and round in the fashion of young men, she wore a shirt, breeches, doublet with hose joined together, long and fastened to the said doublet by 20 points. Long leggings laced on the outside, a short mantle

reaching to the knee or there abouts. A close cut cap, tight
fitting boots or buskins, long spurs, sword, dagger, a brass
plate lance and other arms and style of a man-at-arms. [62]

I was trying to show, earlier in this discussion, that
ideas about witches changed and that Joan of Arc's life
coincides with the intensification of dualism and the pre-
lude to the great witchhunt of the next century. In keep-
ing with my desire to emphasize change in history over
time, while at the same time making connections that
span great divisions and intervals, I would like to turn
now to the maleness of Joan of Arc in later hagiography
and imagery, and show how she has been at the centre of
the rising appreciation of the chivalrous and de-sexed girl,
how the legend of Joan the Maid helped carry the day for
that side of Judaeo-Christian mythology that favoured
adopted masculinity for girls, admired tomboys and ama-
zons, and believed that the denial of the feminine body
and its god-ordained function of procreation was holy
rather than unholy. [63] I think it would be true to say
that if the judges at Rouen had found Joan of Arc guilty
of heresy on the grounds of her activities beneath the
fairy tree, rather than insisting on the diabolical character
of her cross-dressing, she could not have emerged as the
paradigm of female heroism or a national figurehead.
What appeared to learned men a heinous travesty of
nature and divine order in 1431 was slowly developing
into a sign of virtue – the amazon was on her way to
becoming accepted as the face of female heroism. [64]

This change of value constitutes one of those major
shifts in outlook which historical writing can never fully
explain, and it was accomplished in the last half of the

last century, when the cult of Joan of Arc achieved its primary aim, and she was first declared Venerable, then beatified, and then, at last, in 1921, canonized a saint. [65]

At the rehabilitation trial in 1456, the men who wanted to vindicate Joan still did not fully assert the virtuousness of her male dress, and the witnesses made excuses for her, telling stories about her clothes being switched or even stolen from her cell. [66] Later representations of Joan of Arc avoid depicting her male dress, or even her cropped hair, and merely show her wearing arms; some artists, like Rubens, either chose to ignore these historical aspects of her character, or did not know them. Rubens painted her kneeling at the coronation of Charles VII with a woman's loose hair flowing over her armour. [67]

Princesse Marie d'Orléans, a sculptor, made a statue of Joan in 1840 which stands in Orléans itself and in the house in Domrémy – again Joan wears armour, but a modest skirt rather than the leggings described in the trial. [68] During the First World War, the right-wing sculptor and supporter of the Action Française, Maxime Réal del Sarte, portrayed Joan as a *Magna Mater* or Mother of Mercy – again in a skirt. [69] Popular media like film have made sure the audience understands that Joan was reluctant to part with her natural girlishness, but did so when called to a higher task – in Vincent Fleming's film with Ingrid Bergman (1948), there was a tearful scene when her mother cuts her hair before her leaving home – but this was dropped from the final version of the film. By the 1950s, it was not as necessary as it had been to explain how Joan drew back from her militant vocation with girlish modesty; by this date, the seductiveness and strength of the short-haired girl were already accepted and the scene justifying her haircut was no longer needed to preserve Joan as a pattern of heroic virtue.

However, even while the image-makers quail before the full commitment of Joan of Arc to male dress and haircut, the admirable boyishness of the heroine was gaining moral ground. Possibly the most influential sequence of images of her appeared in a children's book by Maurice Boutet de Monvel (d. 1913), which has been translated into many languages and become a classic of children's illustrated literature. [70] His Joan takes on the elfin and androgynous persona that has become familiar to audiences today from films that were themselves influenced by books, and by Boutet de Monvel in particular. If you compare battle scenes from Marco de Gastyne's film *La merveilleuse vie de Jeanne d'Arc* (1929) with Boutet's pictures, you can see clear correspondences. When Boutet leaps time and shows Joan of Arc leading soldiers of the Franco-Prussian war to the front, Cecil B. De Mille follows suit, setting his epic *Joan the Woman* (1916) as a dream flashback taking place in the mind of a French soldier in the trenches of the First World War who has a vision of Joan of Arc appearing to lead the troops. Similarly, Boutet's illustration to the episode when Joan is nearly raped in prison provides a blueprint for the film treatment of the incident in Victor Fleming's *Joan of Arc*; in the images of the burning, in both Boutet de Monvel and Cecil B. de Mille, the half-timbered, gabled buildings in the market place at Rouen are exactly the same. Boutet's interpretation was pervasively influential, and his childlike, boyish Joan of Arc, who has not reached mature femaleness, recurs in later artefacts in a wide variety of media, reaching a kind of apotheosis with Jean Seberg's *Joan of Arc* in 1957.

Of course changes in fashion have something to do with this new gamine Joan – but cross-dressing no longer even appears to be such today, when skirtless girls in leggings are merely following fashion; and the adoption of male gender in appearance does not run the capital risks that Joan of Arc discovered, nor indeed open up a wealth of possibilities or give access to articulate power to the same degree. Nevertheless, her heresy consisted of her defiance in this matter, and her subsequent innocence – even holiness – has also been identified with it; because manliness and grace were always bound up together as a site of virtue, the chief question was, Could a girl be allowed to enter it and tap its latent power? Joan of Arc, in her life and her dress, became a test case, and at first the answer came back that a girl could not put on manliness and grace in this way without devilry; but attitudes changed, and the cult of Joan of Arc reveals that it became possible to assume maleness as a woman with honour and without reproach.

Joan of Arc has been a stirring inspiration to young women, and still is, in many places, today. She is one of the few female saints who led a life of action. She has inspired many women writers and many women campaigners, including suffragists in England and independence and anti-slavery campaigners in America. A woman sculptor, Anna Hyatt Huntington, created a life-size equestrian bronze of Joan as an exalted leader at the turn of the century which still stands in New York near Columbia University. It would be good, I think, to discover in history a male hero, a national leader, a holy man who affirmed female values as coherently as Joan of Arc affirmed male. Gandhi, perhaps. [71] It is interesting that shamans, in the rituals of many cultures, cross-dress in order to deepen their power. [72] Joan of Arc in her lifetime questioned many rules of conformity and broke with convention in unprecedented ways. Yet unfortunately with tragic irony even her cult has developed in such a way that she has become the figurehead for the most entrenched conservatism. [73] French leaders still struggle among themselves to own and control her image as she can be used to confer legitimacy on whatever cause adopts her. Under the statue by Frémiet in Paris there were battles at the end of the last century between the socialists and the Action Française for the patronage of Joan of Arc. The socialists, led by the poet Charles Péguy, declared that she was a woman of the people who represented the people of France, while the right-wing Action Française claimed she represented the king and the faith. There were riots and stonings and all manner of demonstrations regularly in the Place des Pyramides. [74]

History is repeating itself in the 1990s; Le Pen and the New Right adopted Joan of Arc as their figurehead, and began their demonstrations for a 'pure France', free of Jews and immigrants, near the statue of Joan of Arc. I happened to be in Paris on Joan of Arc's feast day in 1990, when we still knew very little about the neo-Right advance in France. I was crossing the Tuileries gardens, when I was approached by a young priest. He was wearing an image of Joan of Arc and I was delighted he asked me to give some money in honour of her feast day. So I asked what it would be used for, and he told me he was recruiting for Le Pen. It is a very sad time in the history of Joan of Arc's cult; it would he a very great loss in what Christine de Pisan called *La Cité des dames*, the City of ladies, if Joan was successfully annexed by the forces of ignorance, intolerance and reaction.

MARINA WARNER

The Trial of Joan of Arc

In 1422 England claimed the French throne on behalf of the young Henry VI. His father, Henry V, had signed a treaty after the battle of Agincourt which would give him the right of succession to the French throne after Charles VI died, but Henry himself died first.

The conflict over the succession split France, the Duke of Burgundy siding with the English, and the loyalists (known as the Armagnacs) supporting the Valois line represented by the Dauphin, Charles. By 1429, England occupied Paris and Reims, and much of the territory north of the Loire. Orléans was under siege, and the Dauphin impoverished.

It was at this bleak moment for the French crown that Joan emerged from her modest background to become a leader and inspiration, instructed by her 'voices' – Saints Catherine and Margaret, she said – to raise the siege of Orléans, to defeat the English in battle, to liberate much of the occupied territory, and to crown the Dauphin at Reims. It was an extraordinary programme, all of which she achieved in about fifteen months.

When Joan was captured by the Burgundians and handed over to the English at Compiègne in 1430 (on a day when she was persuaded to act in a way that did not quite fit what her voices had instructed), she was a great prize for her enemies, who then systematically set about disgracing her. She was kept in brutal conditions in her prison, with soldiers watching her every movement, and, it is claimed, threatening to rape her. In 1431 there was a rigged trial (in which she acquitted herself with great dignity and common sense), accusing her of witchcraft and heresy. One of the signs of her spiritual perversity, it was claimed, was her cross-dressing. After fifteen sessions her judges decided that 'she must be cast forth ... from the communion of the Church as an infected limb' and she was therefore sentenced to death and burned at the stake. In 1456, at the instigation of Pope Callistus III, a commission declared the original verdict had been arrived at by fraud and deceit. A Trial of Rehabilitation was held in which the original trial was condemned. Joan was canonized as a saint in 1920.

The following text is of the first trial.

The Formal Preliminaries

Here begins the report of the trial held by Messire Pierre Cauchon, Bishop and Count of Beauvais, in a matter of faith, against a woman named Jeanne, commonly called the Pucelle, translated from Latin into French [1] by command of King Louis, twelfth of the name, at the request of my lord and Admiral of France, Seigneur de Graville.

First Council

To begin: the said bishop being in the town of Rouen in the year one thousand four hundred and thirty, after the Epiphany, which was the ninth day of the month of January, he had called before him the reverend fathers and masters, my lords Gilles, Abbot of Fécamp, doctor in theology; Nicolas, Abbot of Jumièges, doctor in laws; Pierre de Longueville La Guiffart, doctor in theology; Nicolas de Vendères, Archdeacon of Eu in the Church of Rouen, licentiate in laws; Raoul Roussel, Treasurer of the

[Cathedral] Church of Notre Dame in Rouen, doctor in laws; Robert Barbier, licentiate in laws; Nicolas Couppequesne, bachelor in theology; Nicolas Loiseleur, master in arts, canon of Rouen; all of whom appeared in obedience to the order of the bishop in the Council Chamber of the castle of Rouen.

The bishop informed them that a woman named Jeanne, commonly called the Pucelle, had not long since been taken and apprehended in his diocese; and, that since she was strongly suspected of the crime of heresy, this woman had been delivered and handed over, as much at the request of the Most Christian and Most Illustrious Prince the King of France and England, as at that of our mother the University of Paris, in accordance with his summons and that of the venerable Brother Martin Billon [Billorin], vicar general of the Inquisitor of the Faith in France, in order that inquiry might be made into the crimes and evils of which she has been accused; and that he, being desirous of giving honour and praise to God, and [for] the exaltation of the holy Catholic Faith, might proceed juridically in this matter according to law. Since the Archiepiscopal See was then vacant, he had obtained from my lords of the Chapter permission and leave to proceed in the territory of Rouen to the inquisitions and inquiries which must be made into the said crimes, as is contained in the letters upon the matter. These he exhibited, together with the copies of the letters which the members of the University of Paris had written to Messire Jean de Luxembourg, who [had] held the Pucelle prisoner; together with the schedule of the summons which had been issued to him, copies of which are hereinbefore written.

Second Council

On Monday the nineteenth day of February there appeared before the Bishop of Beauvais, in the house of Maître Jean Rubbe, canon of Rouen, my lords the Abbot of Fécamp, Maître Jean Beaupère, Guillaume Hecton, Jacques de Touraine, Nicolas Midi, Nicolas de Venderès, Pierre Maurice, Gerard Feuillet, Thomas de Courcelles and Nicolas Loiseleur.

The bishop explained to them that a woman named Jeanne called the Pucelle, who was accused of invoking devils and other crimes, had been delivered and handed over to him from the Very Illustrious Prince the King of France and England; and that, since she had been handed over, articles concerning the Catholic Faith had been composed, upon which articles they had examined a number of witnesses, as one could see from the reading of the articles and the depositions of the witnesses who had been examined upon them. These articles and depositions were read in the presence of the above-mentioned persons. After the reading was done, since the Grand Inquisitor of the Faith was not in the town of Rouen, but only his deputy was there, it was ordered and directed by the bishop that the deputy should be called; and that in the presence of notaries he should be summoned to hear read the articles and informations which had been made concerning the crimes and evil-doing of the said Jeanne, and the scandal which had thereby arisen.

And afterwards, by the advice of those who were present, the bishop ordered that this woman should be summoned to be questioned in a matter of faith. This being done, all those present swore to keep secret everything that might transpire in this matter.

Third Council

The same day after dinner, about four o'clock in the evening, the bishop summoned and required the venerable Brother Jean Le Maître, deputy of the Inquisitor of the Faith, who had been called to take part in the trial, and requested him to join with him in proceeding in the matter of the said Jeanne, offering to inform him of everything that had been done at the trial [up till then]. Le Maître answered that, if his commission and deputyship were sufficient, then willingly would he do all he should and could in the said enquiry.

This was done at the lodging of the bishop, in the presence of Jean Massieu, Brother Simon de Paris, Boisguillaume and Manchon.

Fourth Council

On Tuesday the twentieth day of February there appeared before the bishop, the said Beaupère, de Touraine, Midi, Venderès, Maurice, Gerard and de Courcelles, Maître Jean Le Maître, Martin Ladvenu and Nicolas Loiseleur.

The bishop said and declared that he had seen the commission and deputyship of Le Maître, which was good and sufficient, and that he had found from advice that the said Le Maître, deputy, could join with him in conducting the trial. But that notwithstanding this he found from advice that he ought to summon the Grand Inquisitor, if he should be in Normandy, to come to this city of Rouen to be present at the trial, or to commission a deputy in the matter which has been mentioned, who would have full powers to proceed in it.

Le Maître answered that he did not wish to interfere in the matter, as much for scruples of conscience as for the safer conduct of the trial. And furthermore, that, inasmuch as [he was acting as] Grand Inquisitor, to whom reference has been made, he said that he agreed that the bishop could commission whom he please to be present in the place of the Inquisitor, until he be advised whether the vicariate and commission that he has be sufficient to enable him to join in the affair.

After these words, the bishop offered him the [records of the] trial, and all that had been done.

The Preparatory Interrogations

[*These interrogations were intended to produce proofs in support of the Indictment. The Roman numerals in square brackets refer to the number of the Article of the Indictment in support of which Jeanne's answer was included in the promoter's notes.*]

First public session
The following day, which was Wednesday the twenty-first day of February, in the chapel royal of the castle of Rouen, in the presence of the bishop and of my lords and masters, my lord Gilles, Abbot of Fécamp, Jean Beaupère, Jean de Châtillon, Jacques le Tessier, Nicolas Midi, Gerard Feuillet, Guillaume Haiton, Thomas de Courcelles and Maître Richard Praty, were read the letters of the King of England wherein he commanded the ordinary judges of Rouen to hand over and deliver the Pucelle to the bishop to be tried; the letters of the Chapter of Rouen showing that they had given permission to the bishop to hold the trial within the territory of Rouen; and the citation to the Pucelle to appear before him, together with the account of him who had cited her.

These being read, Maître Jean Estivet, appointed promoter at the trial by the bishop, required the Pucelle to be brought and questioned in accordance with law. Which was granted by the bishop.

And since Jeanne had made a supplication that she might be allowed to hear Mass, the bishop said that he had consulted with several wise and notable persons, on whose advice he had come to the conclusion that, in view of the crimes of which she was accused, and of the fact that she wore man's dress, they ought to defer this request: and thus he declared it.

Very soon after, Jeanne was led in to the presence of the bishop and the assessors afore-mentioned.

She being present, the judge spoke to her and explained that she had been taken within the boundaries of his diocese. And since there was common report of a number of her deeds which were contrary to our faith, not only within the realm of France but in all the States in which they were known and published, and since she was accused of heresy, she had been handed over to him to be tried in a matter of faith.

After these words, the promoter showed how at his request she had been cited and convened to answer in a matter of faith, as appeared from the letters and acts which he then exhibited, begging that she should be adjured to speak the truth, and then questioned upon the accusations that he would deliver.

This was granted by the bishop and the court.

This request being granted, as has been said, the bishop caused Jeanne to come before him, and charitably admonished her.

And told her that she should tell the truth concerning

the things which would be asked her, as much for the shortening of her trial as for the unburdening of her conscience, without subterfuge or craft; and that she should swear on the Holy Gospels to tell the truth concerning everything she should be asked.

Jeanne answered: I do not know on what you may wish to question me. Perhaps you may ask such things as I will not answer.

Whereupon the bishop said to her:

You will swear to tell the truth about whatever you are asked concerning the Catholic Faith, and all else that you may know.

To Which Jeanne answered that concerning her father and mother, and concerning everything she had done since she took the road for France; [2] she would willingly swear. But as for revelations sent her from God, never had she told or revealed them save to Charles, who she said was her king. And if they cut her head off, she would not reveal them; for she knew from her visions that she must keep them secret. But within eight days she would know if she ought to reveal them.

After these words the bishop admonished her, and asked her to take the oath to tell the truth concerning the faith.

Jeanne knelt down, her two hands on the book, that is to say a missal, and swore that she would tell the truth in all matters asked her concerning the Faith. But that, about the aforesaid revelations, she would not tell anyone.

The same day, after several questions had been put to her concerning the name of her father and mother, the place where she was born, and her age, Jeanne complained of the fetters which she had on her legs.

She was told by the bishop that several times she had endeavoured to escape from her prisons, wherefore, in order that she might be kept the more securely, he had ordered that she should be fettered.

To which Jeanne answered that it was true that on these previous occasions she would have much liked to escape from prison, as was lawful for every prisoner. She said further that if she had been able to escape, no one could have said that she had broken faith, for she had never given her parole to anyone.

On account of this answer, the bishop ordered John Rice, John Bernard, and William Talbot, [3] to whom the guardianship of Jeanne was committed, that they should guard her strictly, and that they should not allow anyone to speak to her unless they had his express permission; and made the guards place their hands on the missal, upon which they took a solemn oath to do all that they had been ordered.

The same day, Jeanne, being questioned as to her name and surname,

Answered that, in the place where she was born, she was called Jeannette, and in France, Jeanne; of a surname she knew nothing.

Questioned as to the place of her birth,

She answered that she was born in a village called Domrémy de Greux, and in Greux is the principal church.

Questioned as to the name of her father and mother,

She answered that her father was named Jacques Tart and her mother Ysabeau.

Questioned as to where she had been baptised,

She answered that it was in the church of Domrémy.

Questioned as to who were her godfathers and god-mothers,

She answered that they were a woman named Agnes and another called Jeanne; and a man called Jean Bavent was her godfather. She said also that she had heard her mother say that she had other godfathers and godmothers as well as these.

Questioned as to who was the priest who baptised her,

She answered that he was called Messire Jean Nynet [Minet], to the best of her belief.

Questioned as to whether the said Nynet was still alive,

She answered yes, to the best of her belief.

Questioned as to how old she was,

She answered that she was nineteen or thereabouts. She said also that her mother taught her the *Pater Noster*, *Ave Maria* and *Credo*; and that no one else save her mother taught her her faith.

Being required to repeat the *Pater Noster* and *Ave Maria*,

She answered that she would say it willingly, provided that my lord Bishop of Beauvais, who was present, would hear her confession. And although she was several times required to say the *Pater Noster* and *Ave Maria*, she answered that she would not say them unless the bishop would hear her in confession.

And then the bishop said: I will give you one or two notable persons of this company to whom you will say your *Pater Noster* and *Ave Maria*,

To which she answered: I will not say them at all, if they do not hear me in confession.

Second session

The year one thousand four hundred and thirty, the twenty-second day of February. In the Hall [4] of the castle of Rouen, there were assembled together with the bishop, the reverend fathers, lords and masters, the Abbot of Fécamp, Jean de Châtillon, Jean Beaupère, Guillaume Leboucher, Prior of Longueville, Maurice du Quesnoy, Jacques de Touraine, Nicolas Midi, Jean de Fave, Denis de Sabreuvoys, Jean Lefèvre, William Haiton, Pierre Maurice, Gerard Feuillet, Jacques Guesdon, doctors in theology; Jean Sevestre, Jean Le Maître, bachelors in theology; Maître Raoul Roussel, Nicolas de Venderès; the Abbot of Jumièges; Jean Brullet, André Marguerie, Jean Pinchon, Jean Basset; the Abbots of Saint Katherine, of Cormeilles and of Préaux; Denis Gastinel, Nicolas Couppequesne, Gilles des Champs, Geoffroi du Crotoy.

In whose presence and in that of Brother Jean Le Maître, deputy of the Inquisitor of the Faith, the bishop showed how he had summoned and required Le Maître, as general Inquisitor of the Faith, to join in the trial of Jeanne, offering to communicate to him everything that had been done at the trial.

To which Le Maître answered that he was only commissioned in the city and diocese of Rouen; and since the trial was held before the bishop, not as Ordinary of the diocese of Rouen, but as of borrowed jurisdiction, he was doubtful of joining in the matter. And although he had been doubtful as to joining in the trial, nevertheless, as much in order that the trial should not be null and void, as for the unburdening of his conscience, he was content to be present at the trial since he had inquisitorial powers.

This offer being made, Jeanne was first admonished

and required to take the oath that she had taken the day before to tell the truth concerning all that would be asked her of the crimes and evils of which she was accused,

To which Jeanne answered that she had already taken the oath, and this should suffice.

And she was again ordered to swear to tell the absolute truth concerning everything that would be asked her; assuring her that there was not a prince who could or should refuse to take the oath to tell the truth in a matter of faith.

To which she answered: I did so yesterday. You are burdening me too much.

Finally she took the oath in the form in which she had taken it the day before.

The oath being taken, the bishop ordered Maître Jean Beaupère to question her. In obedience to his orders Beaupère questioned her as follows:

Firstly he asked her if she would tell the truth.

To which she replied: You may well ask me such things that as to some I shall tell the truth, as to others, not. She said further: If you are well informed about me, you would wish that I were out of your hands. I have done nothing save by revelation.

Questioned as to what age she was when she left her father's house,

She said that she did not know the answer.

Questioned as to whether she had learned any craft or trade,

She said yes; and that her mother had taught her to sew; and that she did not believe there was any woman in Rouen who could teach her anything in this matter.

She said also that she had left her father's house partly

for fear of the Burgundians; and that she went to Neufchâteau with a woman named La Rousse; [5] where she stayed for a fortnight. In this house she did the household tasks, and did not go into the fields to keep the sheep or other animals.   [VIII]

Asked whether she made her confession every year,

She said yes, to her own curé. And if he were prevented, she confessed to another priest, with her curé's leave. And she also said that she had confessed two or three times to mendicant friars. And that she received the Body of Our Lord every year at Easter.

Asked whether she had not received the Body of Our Lord at other feasts than Easter,

She answered: Go to the next question. And she said that, from the age of thirteen, she received revelation from Our Lord by a voice which taught her how to behave. And the first time she was greatly afraid. And she said that the voice came that time at noon, on a summer's day, a fast day, when she was in her father's garden, and that the voice came on her right side, in the direction of the church. And she said that the voice was hardly ever without a light, which was always in the direction of the voice.

She said further that, after she had heard it three times, she knew that it was the voice of an angel.

She said also that this voice had always taken good care of her.

Questioned as to what teaching this voice gave her as to the salvation of her soul,

She answered that it taught her how to behave. And it said to her that she ought to go often to church. And later it said to her that it was necessary that she should go into France.

47

And it said to her two or three times a week that she must leave and go into France. And that her father knew nothing of her going.

And with this, it said to her that she must hurry and go and raise the siege of Orléans [x]; and that she should go to Robert de Baudricourt, captain of Vaucouleurs; and that he would give her men to accompany her.

To which she answered that she was only a poor woman, who knew nothing of riding or of making war.

And after these words, she went to an uncle's house, where she stayed a week, after which her uncle brought her to Robert de Baudricourt, whom she recognized, although she had never seen him before.   [XII]

And she said that she recognized him by her voices, which had told her that it was he.

She said further that de Baudricourt refused her twice. The third time he received her, and gave her people to conduct her to France, as the voice had told her.   [x]

[She said also that before she received her king's commands, the Duke of Lorraine asked for her to be sent to him. She went, and told him that she wished to be sent into France. He questioned her concerning his health, of which she told him she knew nothing. She said to him little about her journey, but asked him to lend her his son and some others to conduct her to France, and then she would pray God for his restoration to health. She went to him with a safe conduct, and returned to the town of Vaucouleurs.]

She said further that when she left Vaucouleurs, she took man's dress, and also a sword which de Baudricourt gave her, but no other armour. And she said she was accompanied by a knight and four other men; and that day they spent the night in the town of Saint Urbain, where she slept in the Abbey. [6]

She said also that as for her route, she passed through Auxerre, where she heard Mass in the great church; and that she often had her voices with her.

Questioned as to who advised her to take male dress,

[To this question I have found in one book that her voices had commanded her to take man's dress; and in the other I found that, although she was several times asked, she never made any other reply than 'I charge nobody'. And I found in this book that several times she answered variously.]

She said further that Robert de Baudricourt made her escort swear that they would conduct her well and safely.

She also said that when they left, de Baudricourt said to her: Go, and let come what may.   [XII]

She said that she was well assured that God greatly loved the Duke of Orléans, and that she had more revelations concerning him than any man in France, except her king.   [XXXV]

She said further that it was absolutely essential for her to change her dress.   [XII]

Questioned as to what letters she sent the English and what they contained,

She said that she sent letters to the English, who were before Orléans, wherein she wrote to them that they. must leave. And she said that in these letters, as she had heard it said, they have altered two or three words; for example, Render to the Pucelle, where it should be Render to the king; and where there is Body for body, and Chieftain of war; this was not in the letters.   [XXI]

She said also that she went to her king without hindrance.

Further, she said that she found her king at Chinon, where she arrived about noon, and lodged at an inn, and after dinner went to the king who was in the castle.

She said that she went right into the room where the king was; whom she recognized among many others by the advice of the voice.

She said that she told the king that she wished to make war on the English.   [XVII]

Questioned whether, when the voice pointed the king out to her, there was any light,

She answered: Go on to the next question.

Questioned if she saw an angel above the king,

She answered: Forgive me. Pass on to the next.

She said also that before the king set her to work, he had several apparitions and glorious revelations.

Questioned as to what revelations,

She answered: I shall not tell you yet; go to the king and he will tell you.   [LX]

She said further that the voice promised her that very soon after she arrived the king would receive her.

She said also that those of her party well knew that the voice came from God; and that they saw and knew the voice; and that she knows this well.

She said that the king and several members of his Council heard and saw the voices who came to her; and amongst others, Charles, Duke of Bourbon.   [XXXVI]

She said also that she never asked anything of the voice save at the last the salvation of her soul.   [XLIV]

She said further that the voice told her that she should stay at Saint Denis in France; and there she wished to remain. But the lords were not willing to leave her there, because she was wounded; otherwise she would not have left. And she said that she was wounded in the moat of Paris; of which wound she was cured within five days. [XXXVII]

She said that she had made a great assault on Paris.

Asked whether the day she made this assault were a feast day,

She answered, after being questioned several times, that she believed it was a feast.

Asked if she thought it a good thing to make an assault on a feast day,

She replied: Go on to the next question.

These questions and answers being done, the Bishop of Beauvais postponed the matter until the following Saturday.

Third session

The following Saturday, which was the twenty-fourth of February, those who were there the previous day were convoked and called together by the Dean of the Christendom of Rouen.

The Bishop of Beauvais directed and admonished Jeanne to swear absolutely and without condition to tell the truth. Three times she was thus admonished and required.

To which she answered: Give me leave to speak.

And then said: By my faith, you might ask me such things as I will not tell you.

She further said: It could be that there are many things you might ask me of which I would not tell you the truth,

51

especially concerning the revelations; for you would perhaps force me to say by mistake something that I have sworn not to say. Thus I should be perjured, which you ought not to wish.

Addressing my lord of Beauvais, she said: Beware of saying that you are my judge. For you take upon yourself great responsibility, and you overburden me.

She also stated that she thought it was enough to have taken the oath twice.

Questioned again and again as to whether she would take the oath simply and absolutely,

She answered: You can well do without it. I have sworn twice; that is enough. And I believe that all the clergy of Rouen and Paris would not condemn me save in error.

And she added that she would not have told all in a week.

She said also that, of her coming into France she will willingly tell the truth, but not everything.

As to what was told her, that she should take the advice of those present as to whether or no she should take the oath,

She answered that she would willingly tell the truth as to her coming, but nothing more. And that she should not be spoken to any more concerning the matter.

And being admonished and told that she would make herself suspect by her unwillingness to take the oath,

She answered as before.

The bishop ordering and requiring her to swear precisely and absolutely,

She answered: I shall willingly tell you what I know, but not all.   [LX]

She also said that she came from God, and ought not to be here; and said that they should remit her into the hands of God, from Whom she came.   [xxv]

After being again and again ordered and required to take the oath and admonished to do so on pain of being found guilty of the acts imputed to her,

She answered: I have sworn enough. Leave the matter.

And when time and again she was admonished to tell the truth in what concerned her trial, it being explained to her that she was endangering herself,

She answered: I am ready to swear and to say all that I know concerning my trial. But I will not say all that I know.

After saying which, she took the oath.   [LX]

These things being done, she was questioned by Maître Jean Beaupère. Firstly he asked her when she had last eaten or drunk,

To which she answered: yesterday afternoon.

Questioned since when had she heard her voice,

She answered that she had heard it both yesterday and to-day.

Questioned at what time she had heard it yesterday,

She said that she had heard it three times; once in the morning; again at the hour of Vespers; and yet again at the hour of the Ave Maria; sometimes she heard it more often than [this], she said.

Questioned as to what she was doing yesterday morning when she heard this voice,

She answered that she was asleep, and that the voice awoke her.

Asked whether the voice woke her by its sound, or by touching her on the arms or elsewhere,

She answered that she was wakened by the voice without being touched.

Questioned as to whether the voice was still in her room,

She replied that she thought not, but that it was in the castle.   [x]

Asked if she did not thank the voice, and kneel down,

She answered that she thanked it, being seated on her bed. And she said that she joined her hands together, and begged and prayed that it might help and advise her in what she had to do.   [XLIX]

To which the voice told her to answer boldly.

Asked what the voice told her when she was awake,

She answered that it said that she must ask advice from Our Lord.

Asked whether it had said anything before she questioned it,

She said that before she was awake, the voice had said several words to her that she did not understand. But when she had wakened, she understood that the voice had told her that she must answer boldly.   [L]

She said several times to the bishop, You say that you are my judge; consider well what you do; for in truth I am sent from God, and you are putting yourself in great peril.

Asked if this voice had ever varied in its advice,

She answered that she had never found in it two contradictory words.

Asked whether it were an angel coming direct from God, [7] or if it were a saint,

She answered that it came from God.

And added, I am not telling you all I know, for I am greatly afraid of saying something displeasing to it in my answers to you.

And she said further: In this questioning I beg you that I may be allowed a delay.

Asked if she believed that God would be displeased if she told the truth,

She answered my lord of Beauvais that the voices had told her to say some things to the king and not to him.[LX]

She also said that the voice told her that night things concerning the king's good; things that she wished the king to know immediately; and that she would drink no wine till Easter, wherefore he would be happier when he dined.   [XXXI]

Asked if she could make this heavenly voice obey her and carry a message to her king,

She answered that she did not know whether it would be willing to obey her, unless it were the will of God, and that Our Lord agreed.

And that, if it pleased God, it would be able to reveal it to the king; if so [she added] I would be very happy.

Questioned as to why she cannot now speak with her king, as she used to do in his presence,

She said that she did not know if it were God's will.

[XXV]

She said further that if she were not in the grace of God she could do nothing.   [XXXVIII]

Asked if her counsel [her voices] had not revealed to her that she should escape,

She answered: I have [yet] to tell you this.

Asked if this voice has not now given her advice and counsel as to what she should answer,

She replied that if it had revealed or said anything to her [about this], she had not well understood it.

Questioned as to whether, on the last two days that she heard her voices, a light had appeared,

She answered that the light comes before the voice.

Asked if with the voice she sees something,

She answered: I am not going to tell you everything, for I have not permission; and also my oath does not touch that; but I do say to you that it is a beautiful voice, righteous and worthy; otherwise I am not bound to answer you.

For this reason she asked to see in writing the points upon which they desired to question her.

Asked if the voice could see; that is to say, whether it had eyes,

She answered: You may not know that yet.

She said also that there is a saying among little children that people are often hanged for telling the truth.   [LX]

Asked if she knew whether she were in the grace of God,

She answered: If I am not, may God put me there; if I am, may He keep me there.

She said further that if she knew she were not in the grace of God, she would be the most miserable person in the world. She said also that if she were in mortal sin, the voice would not come to her. And she would that everyone might hear them as well as she did.   [XXXIX]

She also said that she thought she was thirteen years of age when the voice came to her the first time.   [X]

Asked whether in her childhood she used to go and play in the fields with the others,

She said she did so sometimes. But she did not know at what age.

Asked if the people of Domrémy sided with the Burgundians or the Armagnacs,

She answered that she only knew one Burgundian,

whose head she would like to see chopped off, that is if it had pleased God.

Asked whether at Maxey they were Burgundians or Armagnacs,

She said they were Burgundians.

Questioned as to whether her voice told her in her childhood to hate the Burgundians,

She answered that ever since she learned that the voices were for the King of France, she did not love the Burgundians. [XXXVIII]

She added that the Burgundians would have war, if they did not do as they ought; she knew this from the voice. [XXXIII]

Asked if the voice told her in her childhood that the English should come into France,

She said they were already in France when the voice first spoke to her.

Asked if she were ever with the other children when they played at fights between English and French,

She said no, as far as she could remember. But she had often seen those of her village fighting against those of Maxey, and sometimes coming back wounded and bleeding.

Asked if in her youth she had a great desire to defeat the Burgundians,

She answered that she had a great desire that the king should have his kingdom.

Asked if she had wanted to be a man when she knew that she had to come [into France],

She said that she had answered elsewhere.

Asked if she ever used to lead the animals to pasture,

She replied that she had already answered; and that, since she had grown up and reached years of understanding, she did not look after them; but she did help to drive them to the meadows, and to a castle called de l'Ile, for fear of the soldiers; but as to whether she looked after them or not in her childhood, she did not remember. [VIII]

Questioned concerning the tree,

She answered that quite close to Domrémy there was a tree which was called the Ladies' tree; others called it the Fairies' tree; and near it there was a spring; and she had heard it said that persons suffering from fever drank of it; and she has seen them going to it to be cured. But she did not know whether they were cured or not. [V]

She said also that she had heard that the sick, when they could get up, went to the tree to walk about; and she said it was a large tree called a beech, from whence comes the *beau mai*; [8] and it belonged to Messire Pierre de Bourlémont. [9]

She said that she sometimes went there with the other girls in summer time, and made wreaths for Notre Dame de Domrémy.

She had heard several old folk say, not of her family, that the fairies frequented it; and she had heard her godmother Jeanne, wife [of the mayor of the village of Domrémy], say that she had seen them there. Whether this was true, she does not know.

She said that she herself had never seen a fairy, as far as she knew, either at the tree or anywhere else.

She said further that she had seen garlands hung on the branches of the tree by the girls; and she herself had hung them there with the other girls. Sometimes they took them away, and sometimes they left them.

She also said that ever since she learned that she must come into France, she played very little, the least that she could. And she did not know whether, since she had reached years of discretion, she had danced near the tree. Sometimes she may have danced there with the children, but she more often sang than danced.

She also said that there was a wood called the Bois Chesnu that one could see from her father's house, not more than a league away; but she was unaware and had never heard it said that the fairies frequented it.

She had heard from her brother that it was said in the neighbourhood that she received her revelations at the tree and from the fairies. But she had not. And she told him quite the contrary.

She said further that when she came before the king, many people asked whether in her country there was not a wood called the *Bois Chesnu*, for there was a prophecy saying that from the *Bois Chesnu* should come a maiden who would perform marvellous acts; but she put no faith in it. [10]   [VI]

Questioned as to whether she wanted a woman's dress,

She answered: If you give me permission, give me one, and I will take it and go. Otherwise no. I am content with this one, since it is God's will that I wear it.   [XIV]

After these questions were done, the following Tuesday was appointed, at eight o'clock. And the assessors were requested to assemble on that day at the said hour, under pain of displeasure.

Fourth session
The following Tuesday, which was the twenty-seventh day of the month of February, following the Sunday of

Reminiscere, in the year one thousand four hundred and thirty, for the fifth session. [11]

Firstly the assessors were convoked; and in their presence Jeanne was required by my lord the Bishop of Beauvais to swear and take the oath concerning what touched her trial.

To which she answered that she would willingly swear as to what touched her trial, but not as to everything she knew.

Many times she was requested by the bishop to answer the truth concerning everything that would be asked her,

To which she answered as before: It seems to me you ought to be satisfied; I have sworn enough.

By order of my lord of Beauvais, Maître Jean Beaupère began to interrogate Jeanne, and asked her how she had been since Saturday.

She answered: You can see that I am as well as I can be.

Questioned as to whether she fasted every day of this Lent,

She replied: What has that to do with your trial?

To which Beaupère said: Yes, indeed, it belongs to the trial.

She replied: Yes, certainly, I have fasted the whole time.

Asked whether she had heard her voice since Saturday,

She answered: Yes, indeed, many times.

Questioned as to whether she heard it in this hall on Saturday,

She answered: That has nothing to do with your trial; and afterwards said, yes.

Asked what it said to her on Saturday,

She answered: I did not well understand it; I

understood nothing that I could tell you until my return to my room.

Asked what it said to her when she was back in her room,

She replied: That I should answer you boldly.

And she said further that she asked advice concerning the things that were asked her.

She said also that when she has leave of Our Lord to reveal it, she will tell it willingly; but touching the revelations concerning the King of France, she will not tell without permission from her voice.   [LX]

Asked if the voice forbade her to tell everything,

She answered that she had still not quite understood.

Asked what the voice said to her,

She said that she asked advice from it as to certain questions that had been asked her.

Asked whether the voice had given her advice as to these matters,

She replied that on certain points she had received advice.

She said also that as to certain questions, they might demand an answer, but she would not give it without leave; and if by chance she answered without permission, she would not have them for warrant. But [she said] when I have Our Lord's leave, then I shall not be afraid to answer, for I shall have a good warrant.   [L]

Questioned as to whether it were the voice of an angel, or of a saint, or directly from God,

She answered that the voices were those of Saint Catherine and of Saint Margaret. And their heads are crowned with beautiful crowns, most richly and preciously. And [she said] for [telling you] this I have leave from Our Lord. If you doubt it, send to Poitiers where I have been previously examined. [XXXIV]

Asked how she knew that it was these two saints, and if she could tell the one from the other,

She answered that she was certain that it was these; and that she well knew the one from the other. [XLV]

Asked how she knew the one from the other,

She replied that she knew them by the greeting they gave her. [XXXIV]

She also said that it was seven years since they first began to guide her. [X]

She also said she knows them because they tell her their names. [XXXIV]

Asked whether they are dressed in the same cloth,

She answered: I shall not now tell you anything else. She also said that she had not leave to reveal it. And if you do not believe me [she added], go to Poitiers.

She said further: there are some revelations which were intended for the King of France, and not for those who question me.

Asked if they are of the same age,

She said: I have not leave to tell you that.

Asked if they talked at the same time, or one after the other,

She replied: I have not leave to tell you that; nevertheless I always receive advice from both of them.

Asked which [appeared] first,

She answered: I do not recognize them at once. I used to know well enough, but now I have forgotten. If she has leave, she will willingly say; and it is in the register of Poitiers. [LX]

She said also that she received counsel from Saint Michael.

Questioned which came first,

She said it was Saint Michael.

Asked if it were long ago,

She answered: I do not speak of Saint Michael's voice, but of the great comfort [he brought me].

Asked which was the first voice that came to her when she was thirteen,

She said it was Saint Michael whom she saw before her eyes; and he was not alone, but was accompanied by angels from heaven.

She said also that she would not have come into France had it not been for God's command.

Asked if she saw Saint Michael and the angels corporeally and in reality,

She answered: I saw them with my bodily eyes, as well as I am seeing you.

And when they left her, she wept and greatly longed that they should have taken her with them.   [x]

Asked in what form was Saint Michael,

I have not yet answered you this; and have not yet leave to tell it.

Questioned as to what Saint Michael said to her the first time,

She answered: You will not have any other answer.

She also said that the voices told her to answer boldly.

She said further that she had not yet leave to reveal what Saint Michael told her; and greatly wished that her examiner had a copy of the book which is at Poitiers, provided that was pleasing to God.

Asked whether Saint Michael and the other saints had told her not to tell her revelations without their permission,

She answered: I will not answer you further about that. And, concerning what I have leave to tell you, I will gladly answer. And [she added] that if they had forbidden her, she did not so understand it.

Asked what sign she gives whereby it might be known that they come from God, and that they are Saint Catherine and Saint Margaret,

She replied: I have told you often enough that they are Saint Catherine and Saint Margaret. Believe me if you will.   [LX]

Asked how she is able to make a distinction between answering certain points, and not others,

She replied that on some points she had asked leave, and on some, she had obtained it.

She said furthermore that she would rather be torn asunder by horses than come into France without God's leave.   [XXIII]

Asked if the voice ordered her to wear a man's dress,

She answered that the dress is but a small matter; and that she had not taken it by the advice of any living man; and that she did not take this dress nor do anything at all save by the command of Our Lord and the angels.

[XII]

Questioned as to whether it seemed to her that this command to take male dress was a lawful one,

She answered that everything she had done was at Our Lord's command, and if He had ordered Jeanne to take a different dress, she would have done so, since it would have been at God's command.   [XIII]

Nor had she ever taken this dress at the order of Robert [de Baudricourt].

Asked if she had done well to take man's dress,

She said that everything she had done at Our Lord's command she considered well done, and from it she expected good surety and good support.

She said also that she had a sword which she obtained at Vaucouleurs.   [XII]

Questioned as to whether in this particular case of taking male dress she considered she had done rightly,

She answered that without God's command she had not done so; and that she had done nothing in the world save by His command.   [XIII]

Asked whether, when she saw the voice, there was a light with it,

She said that there was a great deal of light on all sides as was fitting.   [x]

Asked whether there was an angel over her king's head when first she saw him,

She answered: By Saint Mary, if there were any, I did not know, nor did see one.

Asked whether there was a light there,

She said that there were more than three hundred knights and fifty torches, not counting the spiritual light; and that she rarely received revelations without there being a light.

Asked how her king gave credence to her words,

She replied that he had good signs; and through the clergy.   [LI]

Asked what revelations the king had,

She answered: You will not learn them from me, this year.   [LX]

She said also that the ecclesiastics of her party were of this opinion, that there seemed to be nothing but good in her. [LI]

Asked whether she had been to Saint Catherine de Fierbois,

She answered yes. And there she heard three masses in one day, and then went to the town of Chinon. [XIX]

She said that she told her king on one occasion that it had been revealed to her that she should go to him.

She said also that she had sent letters to her king, saying that she was writing to know whether she should enter the town where he was, and that she had already travelled a good hundred and fifty leagues to come to his aid, and that she had much good news for him; and she thought that the letter also said that she would be able to recognize him amongst all others. [XXXI]

She said further that she had a sword, which, when she was in Tours or in Chinon, she sent to be looked for at Saint Catherine de Fierbois. This sword was in the ground, behind the altar of Saint Catherine, and it was immediately found there, all rusted.

Asked how she knew the sword was there,

She said it was in the ground, all rusted, and upon it were five crosses. This she knew from her voices, saying that she never saw the man who was sent to look for the sword. She wrote to the clergy of the place asking that it might please them to let her have the sword, which they sent her. It was not deep in the ground behind the altar, so she thought, although in truth she was not certain whether it were in front of it or behind, but she believed that she wrote that it was behind [the altar].

She added that as soon as the sword was found, the clergy of the place rubbed it, and the rust fell off without any effort; and that it was an armourer of Tours who went to find the sword. [12] And the clergy of Saint Catherine and the citizens of Tours both gave her sheaths for it. They made two sheaths, one of crimson velvet and the other of cloth of gold. She herself had another made of very strong leather.

She also stated that when she was taken prisoner she no longer had this sword; but that she had always worn it until her departure from Saint Denis.

Asked whether she had ever said or caused to be said a blessing upon this sword,

She said no, nor would she have known how to do so.

She said also that she greatly prized this sword, since it was found in the church of Saint Catherine, whom she much loved. [XIX]

Asked whether she had placed her sword upon any altar,

She said no, as far as she knew, nor had she done so in order that it might have better fortune.

Asked if she had her sword when she was taken prisoner,

She said no, but that she had one which was taken from a Burgundian. [XX]

She added that she had this sword at Lagny, and from Lagny to Compiègne she wore the Burgundian's sword, because it was a good sword for war, useful for giving hard clouts.

She said also that as to where she lost this sword, this had nothing to do with the trial, and she would not reply now. [LXIII]

Asked whether, when she was before the city of Orléans, she had a standard, and of what colour it was,

She replied that it had a field sown with fleurs-de-lis, and showed a world with an angel on either side, white in colour, of linen or *boucassin*; and she thought that the names JESUS MARIA were written on it; and it had a silk fringe.

Asked if these names JESUS MARIA were written at the top or the bottom, or along the side,

She answered that she thought they were along the side.

Asked which she preferred, her sword or her standard,

She replied that she was forty times fonder of her standard than she was of her sword.

Asked who persuaded her to have this design on her standard,

She said: I have told you often enough that I have done nothing save by God's command.

She said moreover that she herself bore her standard during an attack, in order to avoid killing anyone. And she added that she had never killed anyone at all.   [LVIII]

Asked what forces her king gave her when he set her to work,

She answered, ten or twelve thousand men; and that at Orléans she went first to the fort of Saint Loup and then to that at the bridge [the Tourelles].   [LIII]

Asked at which fort she ordered her men to retire,

She said that she did not remember.

She said also that, through the revelation made to her, she was quite certain that she would relieve Orléans; adding that she had so informed her king before she went there.

Asked whether, in launching her attack before Orléans, she told her men that she would receive arrows, missiles and stones from the bombards,

She said no; there were a good hundred wounded, and maybe more. But she had told her men to have no fear, and they would raise the siege.

She also said that during the attack on the fort at the bridge she was wounded in the neck by an arrow, but she was greatly comforted by Saint Catherine, and was well again in a fortnight; nor did she give up either riding or her military command on account of this wound.

Asked whether she knew beforehand that she would be wounded,

She said that she well knew it, and had informed her king of it; but that notwithstanding she would not give up her work. And this was revealed to her by the voices of Saint Catherine and Saint Margaret.

She said also that she herself was the first to plant the ladder against the fort at the bridge; and it was while she was raising it that she was wounded in the neck by an arrow.   [XXXIII]

Asked why she had not concluded a treaty with the captain of Jargeau,

She said that the lords of her party had told the English that they would not have the delay of a fortnight for which they had asked, but that they must go away immediately, and take their horses with them. And for her own part, she told them that they might go if they wished, in their doublets and tunics, safe and sound; if they did not, they would be taken by assault.

Asked whether she had any conversation with her

counsel, that is to say her voices, as to whether or no to grant a delay,

She answered that she did not remember.   [XVIII]

Fifth session

Asked whether she had letters from the Comte d'Armagnac, asking her which of the three claimants to the Papacy should be obeyed, [13]

She answered that the count wrote a letter to this effect, to which she replied, amongst other matters, that when she was in Paris or anywhere else, when she had some time [to spare], she would give him a reply. She was just about to mount her horse when she gave this answer.

After this the letters from the count and from Jeanne were read, and she was asked whether it was her own letter in reply,

To which she said that she thought she had given such an answer, at any rate in part, if not the whole.

Questioned as to whether she said that she knew by the counsel of the King of kings what he ought to believe in this matter,

She answered that she knew nothing about it.

Asked if she were in any doubt as to whom the count should obey,

She said she did not know what to tell him as to whom he ought to obey, for he desired to know whom Our Lord wished him to obey. But as for herself, she held and believed that one ought to obey our lord the Pope at Rome.

She added that she had said other things to the messenger than what is contained in the letter. If he had not gone away so hurriedly he would have been thrown into the water, though not through her.

She said also that with reference to his inquiry as to whom it pleased God that he should obey, she answered that she did not know, but sent him many messages which were not put into writing. As for herself, she believed in the Pope at Rome.

Asked why she had written that she would give him a further answer, since she believed in the Pope at Rome,

She replied that the answer she had given referred to another matter than the three Popes.

Asked if she had ever said she would have counsel concerning the three Popes,

She said that she had never written or caused to be written anything concerning the three Popes. And she swore on oath that on this subject she had neither written nor caused to be written anything at all.   [XXVI]

She said also that before seven years are past the English will have lost a greater stake than they did before the town of Orléans, for they will have lost all they hold in France.

She added, as before, that she knew this by revelation, as well as she knew that we, the Bishop of Beauvais, were there present before her, saying in the French tongue: *Je le sçay aussi bien comme vous estes ici.* [14]

And this she knew by the revelation given her; and that it would come to pass before seven years are past; and she was much grieved that it should be so long delayed.

Asked in what year,

She answered: You will not yet learn this; but I hope it may be before Saint John's Day.

Asked whether she had said it would come to pass before Saint Martin's Day in winter,

She replied that she had said that many events would be seen before Saint Martin's Day; and it might be that the English would be overthrown.

Asked what she had said to John Grey, her gaoler in the prison, concerning Saint Martin's Day,

She answered: I have already told you.

Questioned as to through whom she knew that this would come to pass,

She replied that it was through Saint Catherine and Saint Margaret.   [XXXIII]

Asked whether, since the previous Tuesday, she had often spoken with Saint Catherine and Saint Margaret.

She said yes, both yesterday and to-day; but she does not know at what time; and there is no day when she does not hear them.   [X]

Asked whether the saints always appeared to her in the same dress,

She answered that she [always sees them] in the same form; and their heads are richly crowned; of their other clothing she does not speak, and of their robes she knows nothing.   [XLV]

Asked how she knows whether it is a man or woman who appears to her,

She answered that she was certain it was those saints by their voices, and by what they told her.

Asked what part of them she saw,

She answered, the face.

Asked whether they had hair,

She replied: Assuredly; in the French tongue, *Il est bon a savoir.*

Asked if there was anything between their crowns and their hair,

She answered, no.

Asked if their hair were long and hung down,

She replied: I do not know.

She added that she did not know if they had anything in the nature of arms or other members.

She said moreover that they spoke most excellently and beautifully; and that she understood them perfectly.

Asked how they spoke, when they had no other members, She answered: I leave that to God.   [XXXIV]

She said that the voice was lovely, sweet and low in tone, and spoke in French.

Asked if that voice, that is to say Saint Margaret, spoke English,

She answered: Why should she speak English? She is not on the side of the English.   [XLIII]

Asked who gave her the ring which the Burgundians have,

She answered, her father or mother; and she thought that JESUS MARIA was written on it. But she did not know who had had this written; she did not think there was any stone in it; and it was given to her at Domrémy.

She said also that her brother had given her a ring which we, the bishop, now have; and she requested us to give it to the church.

She said further that she had never cured anyone with any of her rings.   [XX]

Asked whether Saint Catherine and Saint Margaret had spoken to her beneath the tree,

She answered: I do not know.

Being repeatedly asked if the saints had spoken to her at the aforementioned spring,

She replied yes; and she had heard them there. But what they then said to her she does not know.

Being again asked if they had made any promises to her there or elsewhere,

She replied that they did not make any promise to her, except by leave of Our Lord.   [v]

Asked what promises Saint Catherine and Saint Margaret made her,

She answered: This does not concern your trial at all.

Amongst other things, they told her that her king would be re-established in his kingdom, whether his enemies wished it or no.   [XXXIII]

She said also that the saints promised to bring her to Paradise, as she had asked them.   [XLIV]

Asked whether they had promised her anything else, as well as to bring her to Paradise,

She replied that they had made her other promises, but she will not tell them. She said this did not concern her trial.

She said further that within three months she will reveal another promise.

Asked whether the saints had told her that within three months she would be freed from prison,

She answered: That is not in your trial. But she does not know when she will be freed.

She said also that those who wished to remove her from this world might well themselves go first.

Asked whether her counsel had told her that she would be freed from prison,

She answered: Ask me in three months' time, and I will then give you my reply.

She also requested that the assessors should give their opinions on oath as to whether this concerns the trial.

And afterwards, when the assessors had deliberated and come to the conclusion that it did concern the trial,

She said: I have always told you that you cannot know all.

And she added: One day I must be freed. And I wish to have leave to tell you [when]. And for this she begged a delay.

Asked if the saints forbade her to tell the truth,

She answered: Do you wish me to tell you the affairs of the King of France?

She said that there were many matters which did not concern the trial.   [LX]

She said also that she was well assured that her king would regain his kingdom; this she knows as well as she knows us [the bishop] to be present here.   [XXXIII]

She said also that she would be dead, were it not for the revelation which comforts her each day.   [LXIII]

Asked what she has done with her mandrake, [15]

She answered that she never had one; but that she had heard it said that there was one near her village; but that she had never seen it. She had heard it said that it was a dangerous and evil thing to him who keeps it; but she does not know its purpose.

Asked where is the place where this thing of which she has heard [is to be found],

She replied that she had heard that it is in the ground near the tree, but she does not know the spot. But she has heard it said that over the place grows a tree called a hazel.

Asked what purpose this mandrake serves,

She answered that she had heard it said that it attracts money, but she does not believe it, and on this matter her voices have never told her anything at all. [VII]

Asked in what form Saint Michael appeared,

She answered that she did not see his crown; and as to his clothing, she knew [nothing].

Asked if he were naked,

She answered: Do you think that Our Lord has not wherewithal to clothe him? [XXXI]

Questioned whether Saint Michael had his scales, [16]

She replied: I do not know.

She said that she had great joy when she saw him; and said also that he told her, when she saw him, that she was not in a state of mortal sin.

She said further that Saint Catherine and Saint Margaret gladly heard her confession, each in turn.

She also said that if she is in mortal sin, she is not aware of it.

Asked whether, when she made her confession, she ever thought she was in mortal sin,

She replied that she did not know if she were, but she did not believe that she had ever committed such sins. And please God [she added], I never did so, nor will I act in such a way that my soul should be guilty of mortal sin. [XXXIX]

Asked what sign she gave her king to show him that she came from God,

She answered: I have always told you that you will not drag that out of me. Go and ask him.

Asked whether she has sworn not to reveal what has been asked her touching the trial,

She said: I have told you before that I will not tell you anything concerning the king: but that which concerns the trial and the faith, I will tell you.

Asked if she did not know the sign,

She answered: You will not know that from me.

Being told that this concerns the trial,

She said: I will willingly tell you [other matters]; but the things I have promised to keep secret, I will not tell you.

And I have promised, so I cannot tell you without being forsworn.

Asked to whom she made this promise,

She said, to Saint Catherine and Saint Margaret; and it [the sign] was shown to the king.

She said also that she promised them without them asking her, and at her own request; and she said that too many people would have asked her if she had not promised.

Questioned whether, when she showed the sign, there was anyone present save the king,

She answered: I think there was no one but he, although there were a number of people fairly near.

Asked if she saw any crown on the king's head, when she showed him the sign,

She answered: I cannot tell you without perjuring myself.   [LX]

Asked if he had a crown at Reims,

She answered that she thinks that the one he found at Reims he took with pleasure. But a very rich one was brought later. And he did so to hasten [his coronation] at the request of the citizens of the town, to avoid the cost of the men-at-arms; and if he had waited, he would have been crowned with one a thousand times richer.

Asked whether she had seen this richer crown,

She answered: I cannot tell you without being forsworn; and although I have not seen it, I have heard that it was so rich. [LI]

And after these questions were done, the following Saturday was appointed, at the hour of eight in the morning. And the assessors were requested to assemble on this day at the said hour under certain penalties.

Sixth session

The following Saturday, which was the third day of March, for the sixth session, appeared the said Jeanne. And she was required by the Court to swear simply and absolutely to tell the truth in everything that would be asked her.

She answered: I am ready to take the oath as I did formerly.

Whereupon she took the oath on the Holy Gospels.

Over and over again did Maître Jean Beaupère, by order of my lord the Bishop of Beauvais, put questions to Jeanne, repeating to her that she had said that Saint Michael had wings; and yet had not said any thing of the bodies or limbs of Saint Catherine and Saint Margaret.

She answered: I have told you what I know; and I will not answer you further.

She said also that she had seen them so clearly that she was well assured that they were saints in heaven. [XLV]

Asked if she had seen more than their faces,

She answered: I have told you what I know. I would rather you cut my throat [than tell you more].

She said also that everything she knew touching the trial she would willingly tell.

Asked if Saint Michael and Saint Gabriel had natural heads,

She said: Yes, so I saw them. And I believe that it was they, as certainly as I believe that God exists.

Asked whether she believes that God made them with heads as she saw them,

She answered: I saw them with my own eyes. I will not say anything else.

Asked again whether she believes that God made them with heads as she saw them,

She answered yes.   [XLVIII]

Questioned as to whether she believes that God created them in this form and shape from the beginning,

She answered: You will have nothing else from me for the present, seeing that I have answered.

Asked if she had seen or known by revelation that she would escape,

She answered: That does not concern your trial. Do you want me to speak against myself?

Asked if her voices had spoken to her about it,

She said: That is not in your trial. I refer to Our Lord, Who will do His pleasure.

She said further: By my faith, I know neither the hour nor the day. God's will be done.   [LX]

Asked if her voices had said anything in general,

She said: Yes, indeed, they told me I should be delivered. But I know neither the day nor the hour. And [they told me] I must put a bold face on it.   [XXXIII]

Asked whether, when she first came before her king, he asked her if it were by revelation that she changed her dress,

She answered: I have told you; although I do not remember if I was asked.

She said also that it was written down at Poitiers.

[XIII]

Asked if the masters of the other allegiance [17] who examined her, some for a month and others for three weeks, had questioned her as to changing her dress,

She said: I do not remember.

But she said that they questioned her as to where she had taken man's dress; and she told them it was at Vaucouleurs.

Questioned as to whether they had asked whether she took it by [direction of] her voices,

She said: I do not remember.

Asked, when she first visited the queen, if she had asked her about this dress,

She said: I do not remember.

Asked if the king or the queen or others of her party had required her to put off her male dress and take that of a woman,

She answered: That is not in your trial.

Questioned whether she was not so required at Beaurevoir,

She answered: Yes, indeed. And I answered that I would not change it without Our Lord's leave.

She said also that the Demoiselle de Luxembourg asked my lord of Luxembourg not to hand her over to the English.

She said also that the Demoiselle de Luxembourg and

the Lady of Beaurevoir offered her a woman's dress, or cloth to make one, asking her to wear it.

And she answered that she had not Our Lord's permission to do so, and it was not yet time.

Asked if Messire Jean de Pressy [18] and others had not offered her a woman's dress, [XVI]

She answered: Both he and several others have offered me one on several occasions.

Asked whether she believed she would have done wrong or committed mortal sin in taking a woman's dress,

She answered that she did better to obey and serve her sovereign Lord, that is God, than men. [XIII]

She also said that if she had to do so, she would sooner have done it at the request of these two ladies than of any other ladies in France, except the queen.

Asked whether, when God revealed to her that she should change her dress, it was by the voice of Saint Michael, Saint Catherine and Saint Margaret,

She said: You will have nothing else from me at present. [XVI]

Asked, when her king set her to work and she had her standard made, if the men-at-arms and other soldiers had pennons made after the style of hers,

She answered: It is certain that the lords kept their own arms and not [those of] others.

She said further that some of her companions in arms had them made according to their pleasure, and others not.

Asked of what material they had them made, whether of linen or cloth,

She answered: Of white satin; and on some there were fleurs-de-lis.

And she said that she had only two or three lances in her troop; but her companions in arms sometimes had theirs made like hers, only to know their own men from others.

Asked if they were often renewed,

She replied, I do not know. When the lances were broken, they had new ones made.

Asked if she had not said that the pennons made like hers were lucky,

She answered that she had several times said to them [her followers], Go boldly amongst the English. And she did the same herself.

Asked if she had told them to carry them boldly, and they would have good fortune,

She answered that she had indeed told them what had happened and would happen again.

Asked if she had sprinkled or had had sprinkled holy water on the pennons when they were first carried,

She said: I know nothing of it; if it were done, it was not done by my orders.

Asked whether she had not seen it sprinkled,

She said: That is not in your trial. And if [she added] she had seen it sprinkled, she is not now advised to answer you.

Asked if her companions in arms had not put on their pennons JESUS MARIA.

She answered: By my faith, I know nothing of it.

Asked if she had ever carried or caused others to carry cloth of which to make pennons, in the manner of a procession, around a castle [19] or a church.

She said no, and had never seen it done.   [xx]

Asked, when she was before Jargeau what it was that

she wore behind her helmet, and if it was anything round,

She said: By my faith, there was nothing.

Asked if she ever knew Brother Richard, [20]

She answered: I had never seen him until I came before Troyes.

Asked what greeting Brother Richard gave her,

She answered that the people of Troyes sent him to her, as she thought, saying that they were doubtful as to whether she were sent by God.

And when he came near her he made the sign of the Cross, and sprinkled holy water.

And she said to him: Approach boldly. I shall not fly away. [21]

Asked if she had ever seen or had made pictures or images of herself or in her likeness,

She answered that she had seen at Reims a picture in the hand of a Scotsman; and it looked like her in full armour, presenting a letter to her king, kneeling on one knee. And she had never seen or had made any other image or painting in her likeness.

Questioned as to a picture in the house of her host [at Orléans], on which was written JUSTICE, PEACE AND UNITY,

She answered that she knew nothing about it.

Asked if she was aware that some of her party had had Mass celebrated and prayers said for her,

She said she did not know. But if they had held a service it was not at her orders; and if they prayed for her, she is sure that they did no wrong.

Asked whether those of her party firmly believed that she was sent by God,

She answered: I do not know whether they believe it,

and refer to their opinions. But even if they do not believe it, still I am sent from God.

Asked if she thinks that in believing she was sent from God they believed rightly,

She answered: If they believe that I am sent from God, they are not deceived.   [XXI]

Asked if she were not well aware of the thoughts of those of her party, when they kissed her feet and hands and clothing,

She replied: Many people gladly came to see me. And that they kissed her clothing as little as she could help. But she said that the poor gladly came to her, because she did them no unkindness, but upheld and helped them as much as she could.   [II]

Asked what honour the inhabitants of Troyes showed her on her arrival,

She answered: They showed me none.

She said also that, to the best of her memory, Brother Richard was among them at Troyes. But she does not remember if she saw him when she entered.

Asked if he had not preached a sermon when she arrived,

She answered that she only stayed a short time, and did not sleep [there]. And as for the sermon, she does not know.   [LII]

Asked if she were many days at Reims,

She replied: I think we were there four or five days.

Asked if she were not godmother to a child there,

She replied that she was once at Troyes. But at Reims, she did not remember being so, nor at Château-Thierry. But she was twice a godmother at Saint Denis. And she gave the name Charles to the boys, in honour of her king;

and Jeanne to the girls; at other times according as the mothers wished.

Asked if good women did not touch their rings with the ring she was wearing,

She answered: Many women touched her hands and her rings. But she does not know their thoughts or intentions.

Asked who were those of her company who caught butterflies in her standard before Château-Thierry, [22]

She replied that it was never done or said by their party; but that those of the other party invented it.

Asked what she did at Reims with the gloves when her king was crowned,

She answered that gift of gloves were made to the knights and nobles who were there, and there was one who lost his gloves; but she did not say that she would find them. [23]

She also said that her standard was in the church at Reims; and she thinks it was quite near to the altar; and she herself bore it for a short time; and she does not know whether Brother Richard bore it.   [LVIII]

Asked whether, when travelling about the country, she received the sacrament of penance and of the altar frequently, when she was in the good [loyal] towns,

She said yes, from time to time.

Asked if she had received the said sacraments wearing man's dress,

She said yes; but does not remember having received it in armour.   [XL]

Asked why she took the hackney of the Bishop of Senlis, [24]

She answered: It was bought for two hundred *saluts*.

Whether he received them or not she does not know; but there was an agreement for him to be paid. And I wrote to him that he could have it back if he wished [she said], for she did not want it; it was useless to bear weight.

Asked what was the age of the child at Lagny that she went to see,

She replied: The baby was three days old. And it was brought to Lagny to Notre Dame. And she was told that the maidens of the town were before [the statue of] Our Lady; and that she might like to go and pray to God and Our Lady that it might live. And she went there and prayed to God with the others. And finally life appeared in it, and it yawned three times; then it was baptised and immediately after died, and was buried in consecrated ground. For three days, they said, no life had appeared in the child; and it was as black as her tunic. But when it yawned, the colour began to come back. And she was with the maidens on her knees in front of [the statue of] Our Lady, offering prayers.

Asked if it were not said by the town that she had brought this about, and that it was by her intercession,

She replied: I never inquired.

Asked if she knew Catherine de la Rochelle, or had seen her,

She said yes, at Jargeau; and at Montfaucon-en-Berry.

Asked whether she had shown her a woman dressed in white, who she said sometimes appeared to her,

She answered no.

Asked what she said to her,

She answered that this Catherine said to her that a woman appeared, a white lady, dressed in cloth of gold, who told her to go through the good towns, and that the king would give her heralds and trumpets to proclaim that whoever had gold, silver, or treasure should at once bring it forth; and that she would know those who did not and those who had hidden it; and would know where to find the treasure; and it would serve to pay Jeanne's men-at-arms. To which she had answered that she should return to her husband, and look after her household and children. And, in order to be certain of the truth, she had spoken to Saint Catherine and Saint Margaret, who told her that this Catherine was mad and a liar. So she wrote to her king that she would tell him what ought to be done. And when she arrived, she informed him that Catherine was only a fool and a liar. However, Brother Richard wanted them to set her to work, which she [Jeanne] would not permit, wherefore Brother Richard and Catherine were displeased with her.

Asked if she had spoken to Catherine de la Rochelle concerning going to La Charité,

She replied that Catherine did not advise her to go there; saying that it was too cold, and she ought not to go.

She said also to Catherine, who wished to go to the Duke of Burgundy to make peace, that it was her opinion that they would find no peace save at the lance's point.

She also asked Catherine if this Lady appeared every night; and if so, she would sleep with her. And she did so, but kept awake till midnight; saw nothing, and then went to sleep. And when morning came, she asked if the Lady had appeared. And she answered that she had come, but she [Jeanne] was asleep, and she had not been able to wake her. So she asked her if the Lady would come the next night. And Catherine said yes. On this account Jeanne slept during the day in order that she might keep awake at night. And she shared Catherine's bed again the following night, and kept awake throughout the night. But she saw no-one, although she often asked, Will she come soon? To which Catherine answered, Yes, soon. [LVI]

Asked what she did in the moat of La Charité,

She answered that she ordered an assault to be made there. But she neither sprinkled [holy] water nor caused it to be sprinkled.

Asked why she did not enter [La Charité], since she had God's command,

She said, Who told you that I had God's command to enter?

Asked if she had not received advice from her voice,

She replied that she wanted to come into France. But the soldiers told her that it was better first to go before La Charité. [LVII]

Asked if she were a long time in the tower of Beaurevoir,

She answered that she was there four months or there-abouts. And she added that when she learned that the English were coming, she was very angry; and her voices on several occasions forbade her to jump. In the end, for fear of the English, she did jump, and put herself in the hands of God and Our Lady. [XLI] Nonetheless, she was injured. And after she had jumped, the voice of Saint Catherine told her to be of good cheer, for she would recover, and the people of Compiègne would receive help.

She said also that she always prayed to her counsel for the people of Compiègne. [XLVI]

Asked what happened when she leaped, and what she said,

She answered that some said she was dead. And as

soon as the Burgundians saw that she was alive, they asked her why she had jumped.

Asked whether she had said that she would rather die than be in the hands of the English,   [XLI]

She replied that she would rather surrender her soul [to God] than be in the hands of the English.

Asked whether she was not angry, and blasphemed the Name of God,

She replied that she had never blasphemed the saints; and that she was not accustomed to swear.

Asked about Soissons, and the captain who had surrendered the town; and whether she had not denied God in saying that she would have him cut in four pieces,

She answered that she never denied the saints. And that those who had said so were mistaken. [XLVII] For never in her life had she sworn or blasphemed the Name of God or His saints. Wherefore [she added], I beg you, go on to your next question.

[*For the next four days the court collated the results of the interrogations held to date and decided on which points further questioning was necessary. It was also agreed that since owing to their 'numerous occupations' it was impossible for all the assessors to attend future hearings, the task be delegated to a selected few. The bishop decreed that future interrogations be carried out in Jeanne's cell.*]

Seventh session
The Saturday following, being that after the Sunday of Oculi, the tenth day of March, Jeanne was required to tell the truth.

She answered: I promise you that I will speak the truth in what touches your trial. I beg you, do not force me to swear. For the more you force me to swear, the later will I tell you the truth.

She was later questioned by Maître Jean de la Fontaine, by direction of my lord of Beauvais, in this way: Under oath, when you came to Compiègne, from what place did you come?

She answered: From Crépy-en-Valois.

Asked, when she came to Compiègne, if she were several days [there] before she made a sally,

She replied that she came at a secret hour in the morning, and entered the town without her enemies being aware of it, as far as she knows. And the very same day, at evening, she made the sally in which she was captured.

Asked if, at this sally, the bells were rung,

She answered that if they were rung, it was not by her orders, or with her knowledge; and she did not think so. And she did not remember having said that they were rung.

Asked if she made this sally by command of her voice,

She answered that in Easter week last, she being in the moat before Melun, she was told by her voices, that is to say Saint Catherine and Saint Margaret, that she would be captured before the feast of Saint John, that it had to be so, and that she should not be cast down, but take it all in good part, and God would help her.

Asked whether, since Melun, she had been told over and over again by her voices that she should be taken,

She said yes, frequently, almost every day. And she begged her voices that when she should be taken prisoner she might die speedily, without suffering long imprisonment.

And they told her that she should take it all in good part; and that it must happen so; but they did not tell her when; and if she had known it, she would not have gone. And she had several times asked them when; but they would not tell her. [XXXIII]

And then she requested: Go on to the next question.

Asked whether her voices had ordered her to make the sally, or informed her that she would be taken prisoner if she did so,

She answered that if she had known when she should be taken she would not have gone willingly. Nevertheless she would have obeyed them in the end, whatever was going to happen to her. [XXXVII]

Asked whether when she made this sally, she had it from her voices to go and make this sally,

She replied that that day she did not know that she would be captured and had no order [from her voices] to go forth, but she had always been told that she would be taken prisoner.

Asked whether, in making this sally, she had crossed the bridge,

She replied that she went by way of the bridge and the boulevard, in the company of a number of her party, against the people of my lord of Luxembourg. And twice she drove them back as far as the camp of the Burgundians, and the third time as far as halfway there. And then the English, who were there, cut the road between her forces and the boulevard. On this account both she and her men retreated, and during the retreat into the fields on the Picardy side, near the boulevard, she was captured between the river and Compiègne. And there was only the river and the boulevard with its moat

between the spot where she was taken and Compiègne.
[25]   [II]

Asked whether on her standard the world and two angels were painted,

She answered yes.

Asked what significance there were in having on her standard God holding the world, and two angels,

She answered that Saint Catherine and Saint Margaret told her to have it made in this fashion, and to bear it boldly; and to have painted upon it the King of Heaven.

As to its significance, she knew nothing more.

Questioned as to whether she had a shield and arms,

She answered that she never had. [26] But that her king granted arms to her brothers, a shield of azure, bearing two fleurs-de-lis of gold, and a sword between. And she had described these arms to a painter, who had asked what arms she had.

She said that they were granted by her king to her brothers to give them pleasure, without her asking and without revelation.   [LVIII]

Asked if she had a horse when she was captured, and whether it were a charger or a hackney,

She said she was then on horseback, and it was a demi-charger.

Asked who had given her this horse,

She replied that her king or one of his people had given it to her, out of the king's treasury.

And she added that she had five chargers, not counting the hackneys, of which she had more than seven.

Questioned whether she had received any other riches from her king, except the horses,

She answered that she had asked for nothing from her king except good arms, good horses, and money to pay the people of her household.

Asked if she had no treasure,

She replied that the ten or twelve thousand [*écus*] that she had in money was not a great treasure to carry on a war; very little indeed; and that sum her brothers had, so she thought. And she said that what she had was her king's own money.   [LV]

Asked what is the sign that came to her king,

She said it was beautiful, honourable and good, and the richest there could be.

Asked why she was unwilling to tell or show the sign, seeing that she had wished to know that of Catherine de la Rochelle,

She answered that if the sign of Catherine [de la Rochelle] had been as much shown as her [sign] had been to important churchmen, archbishops and bishops – such as the Archbishop of Reims and other bishops, whose names she does not know, and other persons such as Charles de Bourbon, Sieur de la Trémoïlle, the Duke of Alençon, and several other knights, who saw and heard it as distinctly as she does those who speak to her to-day – then she would not have asked to know the said Catherine's sign. Nevertheless she knew through Saint Catherine and Saint Margaret that as for the affair of Catherine de la Rochelle, it was all non-sense.

Asked if the sign still exists,

She replied: Certainly it still exists; and will last for a thousand years and more.

She added that the sign is in the king's treasury.

Questioned as to whether it is gold, silver, a precious stone, or a crown,

She answered: I will not tell you anything else. No man could devise anything as precious as this sign. And in any case the sign that you need is that God should deliver me out of your hands. And it is the most certain one that He could send you. [LI]

She said also that when she was about to leave to go to her king, her voices said to her: Go boldly! For, when you stand before the king, he will have a sign [which will make him] receive you and believe in you. [XXXIII]

Asked, when the sign came to her king, what reverence she made it, and if it came from God,

She replied that she thanked Our Lord for freeing her from the trouble [caused by] churchmen of her party, who argued against her. And she knelt down many times. [XLIX]

She said further that an angel of God, and no other, gave the sign to her king, for which she many times thanked Our Lord.

She said also that the churchmen of her party stopped arguing when they had recognized the sign.

Asked whether the people of her party saw the sign,

She answered that when her king and those who were with him had seen the sign and also the angel who brought it, she asked her king if he were content. And he answered yes. And then she left [him], and went into a little chapel near at hand; and heard it said that after her departure more than three hundred people saw the sign.

She said also that for love of her, and that they might cease questioning her, God was willing to allow those of her party to see the sign. [LI]

Questioned whether she and her king did not do reverence to the angel when he brought the sign,

She said she did; she knelt down and bared her head.

[XLIX]

Eighth session

The Monday after Laetare Jerusalem, XIIth day of March, Jeanne was required by my lord of Beauvais to tell the truth concerning what would be asked her.

She answered: In that which touches your trial, as I have previously told you, I will willingly tell the truth.

And in this manner she took the oath, there being present Maîtres Thomas Fiesvé, Nicolas de [Hubent] and Jean Carbonnier.

Then, by order of my lord the Bishop of Beauvais, she was examined by Maître Jean de la Fontaine.

Firstly, as to whether the angel who brought the sign did not speak to her,

To which she answered yes. And that he told her king that he should put her to work. And that [the country] would soon thereafter be relieved.

Asked if the angel who brought the sign was the angel who first appeared to her, or if it were another,

She said: It is always the same one. And [she added] he never fails her. [LI]

Asked if the angel had not failed her with respect to her good fortune, in that she had been taken prisoner,

She answered that she believed that, seeing it so pleased our Lord, it was best that she should have been captured.

Asked if the angel had not failed her with respect to her spiritual good,

She answered: How should he have failed me, when he

comforts me every day? And she believes that this comfort comes from Saint Catherine and Saint Margaret.

Asked whether she calls them, or whether they come without being called,

She replied: They often come without being called. And other times, if they do not come very soon, she asks Our Lord to send them.

Asked whether she sometimes called them and they did not come,

She replied that she never had need of them without their coming.   [L]

Asked whether Saint Denis had ever appeared to her,

She said no, as far as she knew.

Asked whether, when she promised Our Lord to keep her virginity, she had spoken to Him,

She answered: It ought to be sufficient to promise it to those who were sent by Him, that is to Saint Catherine and Saint Margaret.   [XLIX]

Asked who had persuaded her to cite a man at Toul in an action for marriage, [27]

She said: I did not cite him; it was he who cited me. And there [she added] she swore before the judge to tell the truth; and in fact she never had made any promise to him.   [IX]

She said also that the first time she heard her voice, she vowed her virginity as long as it should be pleasing to God. She was then of the age of thirteen years or thereabouts.   [XLIX]

She said further that her voices had assured her that she would win her case.   [IX]

Asked if she had ever spoken of these visions either to her curé or to any other churchman,

She said no; but only to Robert de Baudricourt and to her king. And she also said that she was never compelled by her voices to keep them secret; but she was greatly afraid of telling about them, for fear of the Burgundians preventing her making her journey; and especially was she afraid of her father, that he too might hinder her journey.

Asked if she believed that she had done well in leaving without the permission of her father or mother, seeing that it is said that one should honour one's father and mother,

She replied that in everything else she had been most obedient to them, save for this departure; but that she later had written to them, and they had forgiven her.   [xlviii]

Asked if when she left her father and mother she believed that she had not committed a sin,

She answered: Since God so commanded, had to obey.

She added that since God so commanded, if she had had a hundred fathers and mothers, and if she had been a king's daughter, she would still have gone.

Questioned whether she had asked her voices to tell her father and mother of her leaving,

She answered that, as for her father and mother, [the voices] were well enough pleased that she should tell them, had it not been for the trouble that they would have caused if she did tell them. For herself, she would not tell them for anything.

She added that her voices left it to her to tell her father and mother, or to keep silence.   [x]

Asked whether, when she saw Saint Michael and the angels, she made any reverence to them,

She said yes; after they left she had kissed the ground on which they stood, doing them reverence.

Asked if they stayed long with her,   [XLIX]

She answered: They often come to Christians who do not see them. She added that she had often seen them among Christian folk.

Questioned whether she ever had received letters from Saint Michael or her voices,

She said: I have not had leave to tell you this.

But within a week from now I will gladly tell you what I know.   [LX]

Asked if her voices had ever called her DAUGHTER OF GOD, DAUGHTER OF THE CHURCH, GREAT-HEARTED MAID,

She answered that, both before the raising of the siege of Orléans and afterwards, every day when they spoke to her, they have often called her JEANNE THE PUCELLE, DAUGHTER OF GOD.   [XI]

Asked why, since she calls herself DAUGHTER OF GOD, she was unwilling to say the *Pater Noster*,

She replied that she would willingly say it. And previously when she refused to say it, it was with the intention that my lord of Beauvais should hear her in confession.

Ninth session
[Monday afternoon, 12 March]
Questioned concerning her father's dreams.

She replied that when she was still with her father and mother, she was often told by her mother that her father had said that he dreamed his daughter Jeanne would go off with the soldiers; and that her mother and father took great care to keep her safely; that they were very strict with her; and that she was always obedient to them save in the incident at Toul, the action for [breach of promise of] marriage.

She said further that she had heard her mother say that her father had said to her brothers: If I thought that such a thing could happen as I have dreamed, I should want you to drown her; and if you did not, I would drown her myself. And that she greatly feared that they would lose their minds when she left to go to Vaucouleurs.

Asked if his thoughts and dreams had come to her father after she had her visions,

She replied: Yes, more than two years after she first heard the voices. [x]

Questioned as to whether it was at the request of Robert [de Baudricourt] that she took man's dress,

She replied that she had done so of her own wish, and not at the request of anyone in the world.

Asked if the voice had told her to take man's dress,

She said: Everything good that I have done, I did by command of the voices.

And she said moreover that concerning this dress she would answer later on; at present she could not do so; but would answer to-morrow. [XII]

Questioned whether in taking male dress she thought that she had done wrong,

She answered no; and that even at this moment if she were with her own people and wearing this male dress, it seemed to her it would be for the great good of France to do as she used to do before she was taken prisoner. [XIV]

Asked how she would have delivered the Duke of Orléans, [28]

She said that she would have taken enough English prisoners to ransom him; and if she had not taken enough for that, she would have crossed the sea and brought him from England by force.

Asked whether Saint Margaret and Saint Catherine had told her, absolutely and without condition, that she would take enough prisoners to ransom the Duke of Orléans who was in England, or that she would cross the sea to bring him from England by force, bringing him back within three years,

She answered yes. And she told her king to allow her to take prisoners.

She said also that if she had lasted three years without hindrance she would have delivered him.

She said moreover that it would have been a shorter time than three years, and longer than one; but she does not at the moment know [exactly how long].   [XXXIII]

Questioned concerning the sign given to her king,

She answered that she would ask advice about it from Saint Catherine.

Tenth session
On Tuesday, XIIIth day of March, in the year one thousand four hundred and thirty,

Being questioned first as to what the sign was, which was given to her king,

She answered: Do you wish me to perjure myself?

Asked by my lord the Vice-Inquisitor whether she had sworn and promised Saint Catherine not to reveal this sign,

She answered: Of my own accord I have sworn and promised not to reveal this sign, since I have been too often urged to do so. So she said to herself: I promise that I will not speak of it to anyone.

She also said that the sign was that the angel, in bringing her king the crown, assured him that he would have the whole and entire realm of France through the help of God and her efforts; and that he should put her to work; for unless he gave her troops he would not so soon be crowned and anointed.

Questioned whether since yesterday she had spoken with Saint Catherine,

She answered that she had. And she had several times told her to answer the judges boldly whatever they asked her concerning her trial.

Asked in what manner the angel brought the crown, and whether he put it on the king's head,

She replied: It was given to an archbishop, the Archbishop of Reims if she was not mistaken.

And the archbishop took it and presented it to the king.

Questioned as to where this took place,

She answered: It was in the king's chamber in the castle of Chinon.

Asked the day and the hour,

She answered: As to the day, I do not know; as to the hour, it was late. She does not remember more; of the month, it was the month of April or March, she thinks; for either next April or this present month it will be two years ago; it was after Easter.

Asked whether, the first day that she saw the sign, her king saw it too,

She replied yes; and he himself received it.

Questioned of what material the crown was made,

She said: It was of fine gold, and it was so rich that I could not describe its richness. The crown signified that he should hold the realm of France.

Asked if it had precious stones,

She said: I have told you all I know.

Asked whether she had held or kissed it,

She said no.

Questioned as to whether the angel who brought it came from on high or from the earth,

She answered: He came from on high. And she understood that he came by Our Lord's command; and he entered the room by the door. [LI]

Asked if the angel walked through the door of the room,

She said: When he came to the king, he did the king reverence, bowing before him, and saying the words that she has already mentioned concerning the sign; and together with this, he recalled the great patience he [the king] had shown in the great tribulations that had come upon him; and from the door he walked across the floor to the king.

Asked how far it was from the door to the king,

She said that she thought about a lance's length; and he went out by the way he came in.

She said also that when the angel came she accompanied him, and went with him up the stairs to the king's chamber, and the angel entered first. Then she herself said to the king: Sire, here is your sign: take it.

Asked where it was he appeared to her,

She answered: I often prayed that God should send the king a sign, and was in my lodging at the house of a good woman near the castle of Chinon, when he came. And then we went together to the king, and he was accompanied by a number of other angels whom no-one could see.

She said further that, had it not been for the love of her, and to release her from the trouble caused by those who opposed her, she truly believed that a number of people would have seen the angel, who did not see him. [29]

Asked whether all those who were there with the king saw the angel,

She replied that she thinks that the Archbishop of Reims, and the lords of Orléans, [30] de la Trémoïlle and Charles de Bourbon saw him. And as for the crown, several churchmen and others saw it, who did not see the angel.

Asked what appearance the angel had, and how tall he was,

She said she had not leave to answer this, but will do so to-morrow.

Asked whether those who accompanied the angel all had the same appearance,

She said that some of them were like each other, and others not, as far as she could see; and that some of them had wings; and some had crowns, and others not; and there were amongst them Saint Catherine and Saint Margaret, who went with the aforesaid angel and the others right into the king's chamber.

Asked how the angel left her,

She replied that he departed from her in a little chapel, and she was much disturbed at his leaving, and wept, and would gladly have gone with him; that is, that her soul would have gone.

Asked if at his departure she was joyful, or frightened,

She said: He did not leave me frightened, but dismayed at his leaving.

Asked if it were on account of her merits that God sent His angel,

She answered: He came for a great purpose, and hoped that the king would believe in the sign, and that they would stop opposing her; and to give help to the good people of Orléans; and also on account of the merits of the king and the good Duke of Orléans.

Asked why she, sooner than another,

She answered: It pleased God so to do, by means of a simple maid to drive back the king's enemies.

Asked if it had been told her whence the angel had brought this crown,

She replied that it had been brought from God; and that there is no goldsmith in the world who could have made one so lovely and so precious. As to whence he brought it, she refers herself to God; she knows nothing more as to whence it came.

Questioned as to whether this crown did not have a pleasing scent, and if it did not glitter,

She answered that she did not remember, but would think it over.

And later on said: It has and always will have a pleasing scent. But he who has it must guard it well. And it has the shape of a crown.

Asked if the angel had brought her letters,

She said no.

Asked what sign the king had, and those who were with him, and she herself, to believe that it was an angel,

She said that the king so believed on the advice of the churchmen who were present, and from the sign of the crown.

Asked how the churchmen knew that it was an angel,

She answered: From their learning, and because they were clerks.   [LI]

Asked about a married priest, etc., and a lost cup, [31]

She said: Of all that, I know nothing, and have never heard it spoken of.   [XVII]

Asked whether, when she went to Paris, she did so by revelation of her voices,

She replied no, but at the request of certain nobles who were desirous of having a skirmish or an assault-at-arms; and she had every intention of going further and crossing the moats. [32]

Asked also whether she had revelations as to the attack on La Charité,

She said no; but she did this at the desire of the captains as she had previously said.

Questioned as to Pont l'Evêque, whether she had any revelation,

She said that after she heard by revelation at Melun that she was going to be taken prisoner, she handed over most of the conduct of the war to the captains; she did not however inform them that she had had a revelation that she would be captured.

Asked whether it were right on the day of the Nativity of Our Lady, being a feast day, to make an assault on Paris,

She answered: It is good to keep the feasts of Our Lady. And, in her conscience, that it was and would be good to keep the feasts of Our Lady from beginning to end. [LVII]

Questioned as to whether she had not said, when before the town of Paris: Surrender the town in Jesus' Name,

She said no; but that she had said: Surrender it to the King of France.

Eleventh session

On Wednesday, xiiith day of March, being questioned firstly as to what was the reason she leaped from the tower of Beaurevoir,

She answered that she had heard it said that the people of Compiègne, all up to the age of seven years, were to be put to fire and sword; and that she would rather die than live after such a destruction of good people. That was one of the reasons. The other was that she knew she had been sold to the English, and she would much rather have died than be in the hands of her enemies the English.

Asked whether this leap was made on the advice of her voices,

She answered: that Saint Catherine told her almost every day that she was not to leap, and that God would help her and those of Compiègne. And she said to Saint Catherine that since God was going to help the people of Compiègne, she wanted to be there. And Saint Catherine replied to her: You must take this in good part; you will not be freed until you have seen the King of the English.

To which Jeanne answered: Truly, I do not want to see him. And I would rather die than fall into the hands of the English.

Asked whether she had said to Saint Catherine and Saint Margaret: Will God allow these good people of Compiègne to die so wretchedly,

She replied that she had not said: So wretchedly, but had spoken thus: How will God allow these good people of Compiègne to die, who have been and are so loyal to their lord.

She said also that after her leap she was two or three days without wanting to eat; and indeed was so injured in falling that she was unable either to drink or eat. Yet she was comforted by Saint Catherine who told her to confess, and beg mercy of God for having leaped, and that certainly the people of Compiègne would receive help before Saint Martin's Day in winter. [33] Then she began to get well and to eat, and was soon cured.

Asked whether, when she leaped, she expected to kill herself,

She answered no. But in leaping she recommended herself to God, and believed that by means of this leap she could escape and avoid being handed over to the English.

Asked if, when she regained her speech, she denied and cursed God and His saints, which according to the questioner is to be found in the evidence,

She answered that she does not remember; and in as far as what she does remember is concerned, she never denied or cursed God or His saints either then or at any other time. And she does not admit this; she cannot remember exactly what she said or did.

Asked if her voices asked her for a delay before they answered,

She said that Saint Catherine sometimes answered at once; and at other times Jeanne had to listen [carefully] on account of the noise made by people, and by her guards. And when she makes a request of Saint Catherine, at once she and Saint Margaret ask Our Lord; and then, by Our Lord's command, they give a reply to Jeanne.

Asked whether, when they come, a light accompanies them; and whether she saw the light when she heard the voice in the castle, and did not know whether it was in the room,

She answered that there is not a day when they do not come to this castle, and they never come without light; and many times she heard the voice, but does not remember whether she saw a light, or whether she saw Saint Catherine.

She said also that she asked three things of her voices: one concerning her deliverance – secondly that God should help the French and watch over the towns which were in their possession; and lastly the salvation of her own soul.   [L]

She asks also that if she is taken to Paris she may have a copy of her questions and answers, in order that she may give them to the people in Paris and say: These are the questions asked me in Rouen, and my replies. And also that she may not be burdened again with so many questions.

Asked, when she said that my lord of Beauvais had put himself in danger in trying her, what was the danger into which my lord of Beauvais and the others had put themselves,

She replied that this was and is what she said to my lord of Beauvais: You say that you are my judge. I do not know whether you are. But I warn you not to judge me wrongfully, for you would so put yourself in great danger. But I warn you, so that if Our Lord punish you for it, I shall have done my duty in so warning you.

Asked what this danger is,

She answered that Saint Catherine had told her that

she would receive help; and she does not know if this is that she will be delivered out of prison; or if whilst she is being tried some disturbance will occur whereby she will be freed. She thinks that it will be one or the other. And furthermore the voices have told her that she would be delivered by a great victory. And later, her voices said to her: Take it all cheerfully. Do not despair on account of your martyrdom, for in the end you will come to the Kingdom of Heaven. This her voices told her simply and definitely, without faltering. And her martyrdom she called the pain and suffering that she was undergoing in prison; and she does not know whether she will suffer still more, but puts all her faith in Our Lord.   [XXXIII]

Asked whether, since her voices have told her that in the end she will come to the Kingdom of Heaven, she believes herself assured of salvation, and that she will not be damned in hell,

She said that she firmly believes what her voices have told her, that she will be saved, as firmly as if she were already there.

And when they told her that this answer had great weight,

She answered that she, too, accounted it a great treasure.

Questioned as to whether, after this revelation, she believes that she cannot commit mortal sin,

She answered: As to this I know nothing; but commit myself in all things to Our Lord.

Twelfth session
The same Wednesday in the afternoon,

As to this question: [34] provided she keeps the vow and promise that she made to Our Lord that she should keep her virginity both of body and soul,

Questioned as to whether there was any need to make confession since she believes, through the revelation of her voices, that she will be saved,

She answered that she does not know that she has committed mortal sin; but if she be in mortal sin, she thinks that Saint Catherine and Saint Margaret would at once abandon her. And she believes, in replying to the preceding question: One cannot cleanse one's conscience too much.   [XLIV]

Asked whether, since she has been in this prison, she has ever denied or cursed God,

She said no; and that on many occasions when she said *Bon gré Dieu*, [35] or Saint John, or Our Lady, those who told about it had misunderstood.   [XLVII]

Asked whether taking a man prisoner and holding him to ransom, and then putting him to death, is not a mortal sin,

She answered that she had never done such a thing.

And when they referred to a man named Franquet d'Arras, who was put to death at Lagny,

She answered that she had agreed to his being put to death since he deserved it, since he had confessed that he was a murderer, a thief and a traitor. She said that his trial lasted for a fortnight; and that the judges were the bailli of Senlis and the magistrates of Lagny. And she said that she had asked to have Franquet [exchanged] for a man of Paris, the seigneur de l'Ours. And when she learned that the seigneur was dead, and when the bailli informed her that she would be interfering with justice in freeing the said Franguet, she then said to the bailli: Since my man is dead, the one I wanted to have, then deal with this man as justice requires.

Asked if she had given or caused to be given any money to him who had taken Franquet prisoner,

She said that she was not the Master of the Mint or the Treasurer of France, to give him money.

And when they reminded her that she had made an assault on Paris on a feast day; that she had taken my lord of Senlis' horse; that she had thrown herself down from the tower of Beaurevoir; that she wears male dress; and that she agreed to the death of Franquet d'Arras; asking her whether she did not believe that she was in mortal sin,

Then the same Wednesday in the afternoon, being the fourteenth day of March, she answered as to the first, concerning Paris:

I do not believe I am in mortal sin, and if I am, it is for God to know it, and for the priest who hears me in confession.

Secondly, concerning my lord of Senlis' horse,

She answered that she firmly believes she is not guilty of mortal sin towards Our Lord, for it was valued at two hundred gold *saluts*, for which he had received an assignment; and in any case it was sent back to the seigneur de la Trémoïlle to give back to my lord of Senlis; the horse was in any case useless to her for riding. And she said that it was not she who took it away from the bishop; and furthermore she did not want to keep it, because she heard that the bishop was displeased at his horse being taken; and in any case it was useless to men-at-arms. And in conclusion, whether he were paid the assignment given him, or whether he had restitution of his horse, she does not know, but thinks not.

Thirdly, concerning the tower of Beaurevoir,

She answered: I did not do it out of despair, but in the hope of saving my life and of going to the help of a number of good people who were in need. And after leaping she made confession and asked pardon of Our Lord. And she believes that she did wrong in making the leap.

She said also that she knew by revelation from Saint Catherine that she had received forgiveness after she had confessed. And it was by Saint Catherine's advice that she confessed it.

Asked if she had been given a heavy penance,

She said that she herself bore a large part of it in the hurt she received in falling.

Questioned as to whether she believed that the wrong she did in leaping was a mortal sin,

She replied: I do not know; but I refer myself to Our Lord.

And fourthly, that she wears man's clothing,

She answered: Since I do so at the command of God and in His service, I do not believe that I do ill; and as soon as it shall please Him to order me, it will be left off.

[XXXIX]

Thirteenth session

Thursday morning, xvth day of March,

After the admonitions were made to her, and she was required to refer to the determination of the Church, if she had done anything contrary to the Faith,

She answered that her replies ought to be seen by the ecclesiastics, who should tell her if there were anything contrary to the Christian Faith; she will be able to tell through her counsel [her voices] what it is; and then will be able to say what her counsel has told her. And in any case if there were anything wrong and against the Christian Faith that Our Lord has commanded, she would not wish to uphold it, and would be very grieved to be opposed to it.

The Church Triumphant and the Church Militant were then explained to her.

Being required that she should immediately submit to the judgment of the Church as to what she had done, whether it were good or evil,

She answered: I will not give you any other answer at present.   [LXI]

Fourteenth session
On Thursday the xvth day of March in the year MCCCCXXX,

Jeanne was questioned on the aforesaid sworn testimony,

And firstly, as to what she had said concerning the manner in which she believed she could escape from the castle of Beaulieu, between two planks,

She answered that she was never a prisoner anywhere but she would escape gladly. And when she was in that castle she would have shut up her gaolers in the tower, had it not been that the porter saw her and caught her. [36]

She said also that it seemed to her that it was not God's will that she should escape that time, and that she must see the King of the English, as her voices had told her, and as it is written above.   [XXXI]

Asked whether she had leave from God or from her voices to escape from prison whenever she pleased,

She replied: I have often asked for it, but so far have not had it.

Asked whether she would go at once if she saw her opportunity,

She said that if she saw the door open she would go, for this would be Our Lord's permission. And she believes firmly that if she saw the door open and her guards and the rest of the English were unable to resist, she would understand that she had permission, and that Our Lord would send her help. But without leave she would not go; unless she made an attempt so that she might know whether Our Lord would be pleased. And she quoted: *Help yourself and God will help you.* And she said this so that, if she escaped, no-one could say that she had gone without leave.

Questioned as to whether, since she asks to hear Mass, she does not think it more proper that she should wear a woman's dress. And therefore she was asked, which she would rather do: wear a woman's dress and hear Mass, or continue in her man's clothing and not hear Mass,

She answered: Promise me that I may hear Mass if I wear a woman's dress, and then I will answer you.

To which her questioner said: I promise you that you will hear Mass if you put on woman's dress.

She replied: And what do you say, if I have sworn and promised our King not to put off these clothes? Nevertheless I say, Make me a long dress, right down to the ground, without a train, and give it to me to go to Mass, and then when I come back I will put on the clothes I now have.

Asked if she would wear woman's dress at all to go and hear Mass,

She said: I will think this over, and then answer you. She further asked, for the honour of God and Our Lady, that she might hear Mass in this good town.

They then told her that she must take a woman's dress, unconditionally and absolutely,

And she replied: Bring me a dress like that of a citizen's daughter; that is, a long *houppelande*, and I will wear it, and also a woman's hood, to go and hear Mass.

But she also begged, with the greatest urgency, that they should leave her the clothes she was wearing, and let her go and hear Mass without changing them. [xv]

Asked if she is willing to submit and refer all she has said and done to the judgment of the Church,

She replied: All my deeds are in God's hand, and I commit myself to Him. And I assure you that I would neither do nor say anything contrary to the Christian Faith; and if I had done or said anything, or there were anything in me that the churchmen could say was contrary to the Christian Faith established by Our Lord, I should not wish to uphold it, but would cast it from me.

Questioned as to whether she would submit to the ordinance of the Church,

She answered: I will not answer you anything further now; but on Saturday send me a clerk, if you do not wish to come yourself, and with God's help I will answer him, and it shall be set down in writing. [LXI]

Asked if, when the voices come, she does them reverence absolutely, as to a saint,

She said yes. And if at any time she has not done so, she has afterwards begged their pardon. And she could not show them as great reverence as properly belongs to them. For she firmly believes that they are Saint Catherine and Saint Margaret.

And she said the same concerning Saint Michael.

Questioned as to whether, since candles were frequently offered to the saints in heaven, she has ever made oblation of lighted candles or such other things to the saints who visit her, either in church or elsewhere; or whether she has ever had Masses said,

She answered no, save in offering one at Mass, in the priest's hand, in honour of Saint Catherine; for she firmly believes her to be one of those who appeared to her; nor has she lit as many as she would have wished to Saint Catherine and Saint Margaret in Paradise, firmly believing as she does that it is they who come to her.

Questioned whether, which she puts candles before the statue of Saint Catherine, she believes that she is putting them in honour of her who appeared to her,

She replied: I do so in honour of God, Our Lady, and Saint Catherine who is in heaven. And I see no difference between Saint Catherine in heaven and her who appears to me.

Asked if she puts them in honour of her who appeared to her,

She replied: Yes. For she sees no difference between her who appears to her and her who is in heaven.

Asked if she always did and accomplished what her voices commanded her,

She said that she obeyed the commands of Our Lord with all her power, which He told her by her voices, as far as she could under stand, and they never command her to do anything save by Our Lord's good pleasure.   [XLIX]

Asked whether in war she had ever done anything without the permission of her voices,

She answered: You have been answered. Read your book [37] carefully, and you will find it.

Nevertheless she said that at the request of the captains she had made an assault at arms before Paris; and she also besieged La Charité at her king's request. And this was neither against nor according to the command of her voices.

Asked if she had ever done anything against their wish and command,

She said that she did and accomplished what she could and knew how to do, to the best of her power. And as for her leap from the tower of Beaurevoir, which she did contrary to their orders, she could not refrain from doing so. And when they saw her necessity, and that she could not help herself, they saved her life and prevented her from being killed.

She said further that, whatever she did in great matters, they had always helped her; and this is a sign that they are good spirits. [XXXVII]

Questioned as to whether she had any other sign that they are good spirits,

She answered: Saint Michael assured me of it before the voices came to me.

Asked how she knew that it was Saint Michael,

She replied: By the speech and language of angels. And she firmly believes that they were angels.

Asked how she knew that it was the language of angels,

She answered that she believed it immediately; and desired to believe it.

She also said that Saint Michael, when he came to her, told her that Saint Catherine and Saint Margaret would come to her, and that she should follow their counsel; for they were ordered to lead and counsel her as to what she should do; and that she should believe what they told her, for it was by Our Lord's command.

Asked how, if the Enemy appeared in the form of an angel, she could recognize whether it were a good or an evil angel,

She said she could easily tell whether it were indeed Saint Michael or a counterfeit in his likeness

She also said that the first time she greatly doubted whether he were Saint Michael, and was then greatly afraid. And she saw him a number of times before being certain that he was Saint Michael.

Asked how she then knew that it was Saint Michael, rather than on the first occasion that he appeared to her,

She said that the first time she was only a child, and was afraid. Since then he had taught and showed her so much that she firmly believed that it was he.

Questioned as to what doctrine he taught her,

She said that firstly he told her that she was a good child, and that God would help her. And among other matters, that she should go to the help of the King of France. And a great part of what the angel taught her is in this book; and the angel told her of the misery that was in the kingdom of France.   [XXXIV]

Questioned as to the height and stature of the angel,

She said that she would answer on Saturday, together with the other answers that she has to give; always providing this was pleasing to God.   [XXXI]

Asked if she did not believe it to be a great sin to offend

Saint Catherine and Saint Margaret who appeared to her, and to act contrary to their commands,

She said yes; but she knows how to make amends; and that she thinks the time she most offended them was in making the leap at Beaurevoir; for which she asked pardon, as well as for the other offences which she had committed against them. [xxxvii]

Asked if Saint Catherine and Saint Margaret would take bodily vengeance for this offence,

She said she did not know, and had never asked them.

Asked why she had said that for speaking the truth one is some times hanged, [38] and if she knew of any crime or fault in herself for which she might suffer death if she confessed it,

She said no. [xxxi]

Fifteenth session

On Saturday, xvii day of March, Jeanne was required to swear to tell the truth.

Asked to answer as to in what form and shape, size and dress Saint Michael appeared,

She said that he was in the shape of a very true and upright man. And as to his dress and the rest she will say nothing more.

As for the angels, she saw them with her eyes; and [the court] would have nothing more from her about it.

She said also that she believes in the deeds and words of Saint Michael who appeared to her, as firmly as she believes that Our Lord Jesus Christ suffered and died for us. And what leads her so to believe is the good counsel, comfort and sound doctrine which he gave her.

Asked whether she is willing to submit all her words

and deeds, either good or evil, to the judgment of our Mother Holy Church,

She answered that, as for the Church, she loves it and would support it with all her power for our Christian Faith; and it is not she who should be forbidden to go to church and hear Mass. As for the good works that she has done, and her coming, she must refer to the King of Heaven, Who sent her to Charles, son of Charles King of France, who will himself be King of France.

And you will see [she added], that the French will soon win a great action which God will send to them; so much so that it will shake almost the whole realm of France.

And she stated that she says this, so that, when it comes to pass, it may be remembered that she said it.

And being asked to say when,

She said: In this I refer to Our Lord.

Asked to say whether she will submit to the decision of the Church,

She answered: I refer in this to Our Lord Who sent me, to Our Lady and to all the blessed saints in heaven.

And it is her opinion that the Church and Our Lord are one; and that they ought not to make difficulties seeing that they are one.

Then she was told that there is the Church Triumphant, where are God, the saints, and the souls that are saved; and there is the Church Militant, that is to say our Holy Father the Pope, God's Vicar upon earth, the cardinals, the prelates of the Church, and the clergy, and all good Catholic Christians; and this Church when assembled cannot err, and is governed by the Holy Spirit.

Wherefore, being asked if she will not submit to the Church Militant, as it has been explained to her,

She answered that it was from God, from the Virgin Mary, and from all the blessed saints in heaven, and from the Church Triumphant on high, and by their commands, that she came to the King of France. And to this Church she submits all her good deeds, and everything that she has done or is to do. [xxv]

And in answer to whether she would submit to the Church Militant,

She said that she would not now make any other answer.

Asked what she says as to the woman's dress that they offered her in order that she might go and hear Mass,

She said that as to the woman's dress, she would not take it yet; not till it pleased Our Lord. And if it must be that she is found guilty, then she begs the lords of the Church to grant her the grace of a woman's dress and a hood for her head; that she would rather die than go back on what Our Lord had commanded her to do; and firmly believes that Our Lord will not suffer her to be brought so low, that she might not receive help from God by a miracle. [xv]

Asked why, since she has said that she wears man's dress by God's command, she asks a woman's dress to wear in her last hours,

She answered: It suffices that it be long. [xiv]

Asked if her godmother who saw the fairies [Jeanne Aubry] is considered a wise woman,

She said that she is considered a sensible and upright woman; not a witch or a sorceress. [v]

Asked whether her saying that she would take a woman's dress if they would let her go, was pleasing to God,

She answered that if they let her go in a woman's dress, she would at once put on man's dress and do as Our Lord commanded her. She has said this before. And she would not for anything take the oath that she would not take up arms or wear male dress to do Our Lord's will.   [xv]

Questioned as to the age and the clothing of Saint Catherine and Saint Margaret,

She said: You have already been answered as to this, and you will have no further reply; I have told you as best I can.   [xxxi]

Asked if she did not believe before to-day that the fairies were evil spirits,

She answered that she knew nothing about it.   [v]

Asked if she knew whether Saint Catherine and Saint Margaret hated the English,

She said: They love what Our Lord loves, and hate what God hates.

Asked whether God hates the English,

She said that as to the love or hate that God has for the English, or what He would do for their souls, she knows nothing; but she is well assured that they will be driven out of France, except those who die there; and that God will send the French victory over the English.

Questioned as to whether God were for the English while their cause prospered in France,

She answered that she did not know whether God hated the French; but she believes that He will allow them to be defeated for their sins, if in fact they are [in a state of sin].   [xxxv]

Asked what warrant and help she expected to have from Our Lord in taking man's dress,

She said, both in the matter of this dress and in the other things she had done, she sought nothing but the salvation of her soul.   [xii]

Asked what arms she offered at Saint Denis,

She answered that it was a suit of white [39] armour, [suitable for] a man-at-arms, together with a sword, and that she won it before Paris.

Asked why she offered them,

She said it was out of devotion, according to the custom of soldiers when they were wounded. And since she was wounded before Paris, she offered them to Saint Denis, that being the war-cry of France.

Asked if it were that they might be worshipped,

She answered no. [LIX]

Asked what was the purpose of the five crosses which were on the sword that she found at Saint Catherine de Fierbois,

She said she did not know. [XIX]

Asked who had urged her to have angels with arms, feet, legs, and wearing clothing, painted [on her standard],

She said: You have already been answered.

Asked if she had had those who came to her painted,

She said that she had them painted in the same way that they are painted in churches.

Asked if she had ever seen them as they were painted,

She replied: I will tell you nothing more about it.

Asked why she had not had the light that came to her with the angels or the voices painted,

She answered that it was not commanded her.

Sixteenth session

On Saturday, XVIIth day of March, MCCCCXXX, after dinner,

Questioned whether the two angels painted on her

standard represented Saint Michael and Saint Gabriel,

She answered that they were there solely in honour of Our Lord, Who was painted on the standard. And she had this picture of the angels made only in honour of Our Lord Who was shown thereon holding the world.

Asked if these two angels who were shown on the standard were the two angels who guard the world; and why there were not more of them, seeing that it was Our Lord Who commanded her to take this standard,

She answered that the whole standard was commanded by Our Lord by means of the voices of Saint Catherine and Saint Margaret who said to her: Take the standard in the Name of the King of Heaven. She had this figure of Our Lord made, and those of the two angels; and as to colour and everything else she did it by their command.

Questioned as to whether she had asked them if, in virtue of this standard, she would win all the battles she fought, and gain the victory,

She answered that they told her to take it boldly and God would help her.

Asked which helped the most, she or her standard,

She said that whether the victory was her standard's or hers, it was all for Our Lord.

Asked whether the hope of being victorious was based upon her standard or upon herself,

She said that it was based upon Our Lord and upon no-one else.

Asked whether, if another carried it, he would have had as good fortune as she had when she carried it,

She answered: I do not know. I refer in all to Our Lord.

Asked whether, if one of the men of her party had given her his standard to carry, and she had carried it, she would have had as great faith in it as in her own which was given her by God, or even as in that of her king,

She answered: I always bore more gladly that which was given me by Our Lord. And in everything I wait on Our Lord. [LVIII]

Asked what was the purpose of the sign that she put in her letters: JESUS MARIA,

She said that the clerks who wrote her letters put them there; and that some said that it was correct to put these two words: JESUS MARIA. [XXIV]

Asked whether it had been revealed to her that if she lost her virginity she would lose her good fortune, and that her voices would come no more to her,

She said: That has not been revealed to me.

Asked whether she believes that if she were married the voices would come to her,

She answered: I do not know; and I wait upon Our Lord.

Asked whether she thinks and firmly believes that her king did right in killing or causing to be killed my lord of Burgundy, [40]

She answered that this was a great tragedy for the kingdom of France; and whatever there had been between them, God had sent her to the help of the King of France.

Asked, since she had told my lord of Beauvais that she would answer him and his commissaries as she would our Holy Father the Pope, and yet there were several questions to which she would not reply, whether she would not answer more fully than she had to my lord of Beauvais,

She answered that she has replied as truly as she knows

how; and if anything comes to her mind that she has not said, she will gladly tell it.

Asked whether it seems to her that she is bound to tell the full truth to the Pope, Vicar of God, about everything they ask her touching the Faith and the state of her conscience,

She said that she demands to be brought to the Church [41] before him; then she will answer everything that she ought to answer. [LXI]

Questioned about one of her rings on which is written: JESUS MARIA; of what material it is made, [42]

She said that she does not exactly know; and if it is of gold it is not of fine gold. She does not know whether it is of gold or of latten; and she thinks it has three crosses, and nothing else that she knows of except JESUS MARIA.

Asked why she looked at this ring with gladness when she went into battle,

She said it was out of pleasure, and in honour of her father and mother; having her ring on her finger, [43] she had touched Saint Catherine when she appeared to her.

Asked what part of Saint Catherine,

She answered: You will get no other reply. [XX]

Asked if she had ever kissed or embraced Saint Catherine or Saint Margaret,

She said she had embraced them both.

Asked whether they smelt pleasant,

She replied: Assuredly they did so.

Asked whether in embracing them she felt warmth or anything else,

She said she could not embrace them without feeling and touching them.

Asked what part she embraced, whether the upper or lower,

She answered: It is more fitting to embrace them above rather than below. [44]   [XLII]

Asked if she had not given them garlands,

She answered that she had often given them, in their honour, to their pictures or statues in churches; but to those who appeared to her she had never given such, as far as she could remember.

Asked, when she hung garlands on the tree, did she put them there in honour of those who appeared to her,

She said no.

Asked whether, when her saints came to her, she made them any reverence such as kneeling to them or bowing,

She said yes.

And the more she could show them reverence, the more she did so. For she knows that these are they who are in the Kingdom of Heaven.   [XLIX]

Asked whether she knows anything of those who consort with the fairies,

She answered that she herself never did so, or knew anything about it, but she had heard it said that they went on Thursdays, but she does not believe in it, and thinks it only sorcery.   [V]

Asked whether her standard was not flown at the king's side,

She said no, as far as she knows.

Asked why it was brought into the church of Reims at the coronation, rather than those of the other captains,

She answered: It had taken part in the dangers: it was only right that it should also have the honour.   [LVIII]

[On 18 and 22 March, Cauchon, Le Maître and various of the assessors held further consultations as to the preparation of the Articles of Indictment. On 24 March the report of the earlier interrogations was read over to Jeanne, who agreed it to be correct. On the following day, Palm Sunday, she was asked again if she would put on female clothing so that she might hear Mass, but she said that this was impossible for her, and asked to be allowed to hear Mass in her male attire. This was refused. On 26 March, it was agreed that the Seventy Articles be put to Jeanne next day and that, if she refused to reply to any of them, she should be held confessed of the accusations therein. (In the manuscript the text is inverted at this point by the insertion of the proceedings of 2 May. They are here replaced in their correct order.)]

Trial in Ordinary

The exhortation in the prison
On Wednesday, xviiith day of April, mccccxxx,

Maître Guillaume Le Boucher, together with the judges hereinafter mentioned, Maîtres Jacques de Touraine, Maurice du Chêne, Nicolas Midi, Guillaume Dolys, Gerard Feuillet, all masters in theology, and Maître Guillaume Haiton, met in the room in which Jeanne was held prisoner.

The Bishop of Beauvais explained to them that Jeanne had been questioned during several days upon the great and important matter of the Faith, in the presence of several learned clerks; and that the clerks had found several faults committed by the said Jeanne.

And since Jeanne was not able to understand or discern many of the matters contained in her trial, as to what was contrary to our Faith and the doctrine of the doctors of the Church, they offered to give her good and helpful counsel to advise her; asking her to look around and choose any one or more of those present to advise her as to what she should do, and to lead her back into the way of truth. And they offered her the doctors of theology and the jurists who were present.

And they informed her that if she was unwilling to accept counsel and follow the Church's advice, she would be in great danger of body,

To which she answered: It seems to me, seeing the

illness from which I am suffering, that I am in great danger of death. And if it be thus that God desires to do His pleasure with me, I ask you to hear my confession and [give me] my Saviour also, and [that I may be buried] in consecrated ground.

She was answered: If you wish to have the privileges and the sacraments of the Church, you must do as good Catholics should do, and submit to Holy Church.

She said: I am not able to tell you anything more now.

She was then told that the more she feared for her life on account of her illness, the more should she amend her life; and that she would not enjoy the rights of the Church as a Catholic if she did not submit to the Church.

She answered: If my body dies in prison, I trust that you will bury it in consecrated ground. But if you do not, then I put my trust in Our Lord.   [LXI]

She was told that formerly she had said in her trial that if she had done or said anything contrary to the Christian Faith ordained by Our Lord, she would not uphold it.

She answered: I refer to the answer that I have given, and to Our Lord.

Since she had said that she had had many revelations from God, from Saint Michael, and from Saint Catherine and Saint Margaret, she was asked whether, if some good creature came to her and said he had had a revelation from God concerning herself, she would believe him,

She answered that no Christian in the world could come to her saying he had had a revelation, without her knowing whether he was speaking the truth or not. She would know this from Saint Catherine and Saint Margaret.

Asked whether she thought that God could reveal

something to a good creature, which was unknown to her,

She answered: Of course He could. But I should not believe either man or woman unless I had a sign.

Asked whether she believed that Holy Scripture was revealed by God,

She answered: You know this; it is certain that it was.

She was then summoned, exhorted and required to take the good advice of the clerks and learned doctors, and to trust in it for the salvation of her soul.

And the final answer that she gave to the question asked her, whether she were willing to submit her deeds to our Mother Holy Church, was:

Whatever is going to happen to me, I will not say anything different from what I have said.

When they heard this, Maîtres Guillaume Le Boucher, Maurice du Chêne, Jacques de Touraine, Guillaume Dolys and Gerard Feuillet informed her that it was her duty to submit to our Mother Holy Church. And they proved to her, by means of a number of authorities and examples in Holy Scripture, that she ought to obey. And amongst the others, Maître Nicolas Midi, in giving his advice, pointed out to her what is written in the eighteenth chapter of Saint Matthew: If thy brother shall trespass against thee, go and tell him his fault between thee and him alone … and if he shall neglect to hear … tell it unto the Church: but if he neglect to hear the Church, let him be unto thee as an heathen man and a publican.

And finally he told her that unless she would be obedient to the Church, she would be abandoned as a heathen. To which Jeanne answered that she was a good Christian, and had been baptised so. And that she would die a good Christian.

Asked whether, since she demanded that the Church should administer her Creator [to her], she was willing to submit to the Church, and if so they would promise to administer It,

She answered that as to submission, she would not reply in any other way than that in which she has done; that she loves God; and that she would help and uphold the Church with all her power. [LXI]

Asked if she would not like a fine and notable procession [45] to be ordered to bring her to a good estate, if she were not therein,

She answered that she would greatly like good Catholics to pray God for her.

The public admonition

The same day [46] Jeanne was brought before the judges in this trial.

The bishop, in their presence, admonished her that she should follow the advice and admonitions which had been given to her by Maître Jean de Châtillon, doctor in theology, for the salvation both of her soul and her body, and if she were unwilling so to do, she would fall into grave danger both of body and soul.

And then the judges begged de Châtillon to proceed charitably to the said admonitions.

To which de Châtillon answered that he would gladly do so.

Firstly, he pointed out to her that all loyal Christians are obliged to believe and hold the articles of the Faith.

And he showed her the form and manner thereof, as she had previously been shown.

He then asked her whether she was willing to correct

herself and amend her faults in accordance with the deliberation.

To which she answered: Read your book.

That is to say, the schedule which the bishop [47] was holding.

And then I will answer you. I wait upon God my Creator in all. I love Him with all my heart.

Questioned as to whether she desires to answer to this general admonition,

She answered: I trust in my judge, that is the King of Heaven and earth.

She was then told: Formerly you said that your deeds were seen and cross-examined, as is contained in the schedule.

She answered that she gives the same answer now.

When it was explained to her what the Church Militant meant, and [she was] admonished to believe and hold the article *Unam Sanctam Ecclesiam*, etc., and to submit to the Church Militant,

She answered: I believe in the Church on earth; but for my deeds and words, as I have previously said, I refer the whole matter to God Who caused me to do what I have done.

She said also that she submits to God her Creator, Who caused her to do what she did; and refers it to Him in His own Person.

Asked if she means that she has no judge on earth, and our Holy Father the Pope is not her judge,

She replied: I will tell you nothing else. I have a good Master, Our Lord, in Whom I trust for everything, and not in any other.

She was told that if she did not wish to believe in the

Church and in the article *Ecclesiam Sanctam Catholicam*, she would be a heretic to uphold [her views], and that she would be punished by other judges who would sentence her to be burned.

She answered: I will tell you nothing else. And [even] if I saw the fire, I should tell you what I have told you, and nothing else.

Questioned as to whether, if the General Council, that is to say our Holy Father, the Cardinals [and the rest] were here, she would be willing to submit,

She answered: You will drag nothing else from me.

Asked if she is willing to submit to our Holy Father the Pope,

She said: Bring me to him, and I shall answer him.

She was unwilling to answer further,

Concerning her dress, etc.

She answered that in the matter of her clothing, she was most willing to wear a long dress and a woman's hood in which to go to church and receive her Saviour, as she has previously said; provided that immediately afterwards she may take it off and put on again that which she is wearing.

It was also explained to her that in the matter of her taking man's dress, there was now no necessity [for her to continue to do so], and especially since she was in prison,

She answered: When I shall have done that for which I have been sent by God, I shall take a woman's dress.

Asked if she believes she does well to wear male dress,

She answered: I trust in Our Lord.

Questioned on the explanation that she was given, that is on her saying that she did well and did not sin in wearing the said dress, together with the circumstances touching the fact of taking and wearing this dress, and in saying that God and the saints made her do so, she was guilty of blasphemy, and, as is more fully contained in the schedule, she erred and did evil,

She answered that she blasphemed neither God nor His saints.

Being admonished to leave off wearing this dress, and to cease believing that she did well to wear it; and being ordered to take a woman's dress,

She answered that she would not do otherwise.

Asked whether, every time that Saint Catherine and Saint Margaret come, she signs herself,

She answered that sometimes she makes the sign of the Cross, and other times she does not.

Concerning the revelations,

She answered that in this matter she refers to her judge, that is to say, God. And she says that her revelations come from God, without any intermediary.

Asked whether, concerning the sign given to her king, she would refer to the Archbishop of Reims, the elder de Boussac, and to the knights de Bourbon, de la Trémoïlle and la Hire, to whom or to one of whom she said she had formerly shown this crown, they being present when the angel brought the crown and gave it to the archbishop, or if she would refer to others of her party, who would write under their seals of what they know,

She said: Send a messenger, and I will write to them all about this trial.

And otherwise she would neither believe nor refer to them.

As to her rash faith [in prophesying future events],

She answered: I refer to my judge, that is, God; and

to what I have previously said, which is in the book.

Asked, if they gave her two, three or four knights [48] of her party, who would come under a safe conduct, whether she would be willing to refer herself to them concerning her apparitions and the matters contained in this trial,

She said, let them come, and then she would answer. Otherwise she was not willing to refer herself or submit herself in this trial.

Asked whether in the church of Poitiers, where she was examined, she was willing to refer and submit herself,

She answered: Do you think you can catch me that way, and draw me to you?

In conclusion, she was abundantly and newly admonished to submit to the Church, under pain of being abandoned by the Church. And if the Church abandoned her, she would be in great danger both of body and soul; her soul in peril of everlasting fire, and her body in danger of the flames of this world, by the sentence of other judges,

To which she answered: You will not do as you say against me without suffering evil, both of body and soul.

Asked to give one reason why she will not submit to the Church,

She will give no other answer.

And afterwards, a number of doctors of different sciences and faculties admonished and charitably exhorted her to submit to the Universal Church Militant and to the General Council; explaining to her the peril and danger to which she exposed herself as much in body as in soul, if she does not submit to the Church Militant.

To which she answered as before.

Finally the bishops told her that she should think well

and advisedly over these monitions, and that she should
change her mind.

To which Jeanne answered: How long do you give me
to think it over?

The bishop told her that she must do so immediately,
and that she should answer as she wished.

And at that time nothing further was done.

The threat of torture

On the Wednesday, ixth of May, in the great dungeon
of the castle of Rouen,

Jeanne was led into the presence of her judges, who
were accompanied by Maîtres Jean de Châtillon,
Guillaume Erard, the Abbot of Saint Cornille, Guillaume
Eston, André Marguerie, Nicolas de Venderès, Aubert
Morel, Nicolas Loiseleur and Messire Jean Massieu,
Dean of the Christendom of Rouen.

The monitions and exhortations being done, [49]

Jeanne replied to the judges and assessors: Truly, if you
were to tear me limb from limb and make my soul leave
my body, I would not say to you anything else. [And if you
force me to do so], then afterwards I shall say that you
made me say so by force.

She said also that on Holy Cross Day [50] she received
comfort from Saint Gabriel. And that her voices had told
her that it was Saint Gabriel.

She said further that she had asked them whether she
ought to submit to the Church, since the churchmen were
pressing her strongly to do so, and they told her that if she
wished Our Lord to help her, she should wait on Our
Lord for all her deeds.

She said that she well knew that Our Lord was always

master of her deeds; and that the Enemy never had power over them.

Furthermore she said that she had asked Saint Michael and her other voices if she would be burned; and that the voices had told her that she must wait on Our Lord and He would help her.

Concerning the sign of the crown which she said had been given to the Archbishop of Reims, being asked whether she wished him to be consulted about it,

She answered: Have him come here, that I may hear him speak; then I shall answer you. He would not dare to tell you the contrary of what I have said to you.

Deliberation as to torture

The XIIth day of May, in the house of my lord the Bishop of Beauvais, at the hour of Vespers,

The judges being assembled in the presence of the Vice-Inquisitor of the Faith: Maître Raoul Roussel, Treasurer of the [Cathedral] Church of Rouen, Nicolas de Venderès, archdeacon, André Marguerie, Guillaume Erard, doctors in theology, Robert Barbery, Denis Gastinel, Aubert Morel, Thomas de Courcelles, Nicolas Couppequesne, Jean le Doulx, Ysambard de la Pierre, and Nicolas Loiseleur, jurists.

After they had been told what had been done the previous Wednesday, they were asked what still remained to be done; and whether it were expedient to put Jeanne to the torture.

They answered as follows: Firstly, Maître Raoul Roussel said no; in order that the trial which had been held could not be calumniated.

Maître Nicolas de Venderès said that it was not expedient to put her to the torture as yet.

Maître André Marguerie said that it was not expedient at the moment.

Maître Guillaume Erard, in no circumstances should she be put to the torture; that the matter was clear enough without torture.

Maître Robert Barbery said as the afore-mentioned. But that she should again be admonished, once for all; and then, if she was unwilling to submit to the Church, one should proceed otherwise.

Maître Denis Gastinel said that it was not expedient to put her to the torture in order to know the truth of her falsehoods.

Maître Thomas de Courcelles said that it seemed to him she ought to be put to the torture; [51] and that she should be questioned as to whether she would submit to the judgment of the Church.

Maître Nicolas Couppequesne said it is not expedient that she should be put to the torture; and that she should be admonished time and again to submit to the Church's judgment.

Maître Jean le Doulx said the same as Couppequesne.

Brother Ysambard de la Pierre, as the above; but that she should still be admonished to submit herself to the Church Militant.

Maître Nicolas Loiseleur said that it seemed to him that, for her [soul's] health, she should be put to the torment; but that nevertheless he would stand by the opinion of those who had previously [given their views].

Maître Guillaume Haiton, who arrived later, was of the opinion that she ought not to be put to the torture.

Maître Jean Le Maître, Vice-Inquisitor, was of the opinion that she should be questioned frequently, to know if she would be willing to submit to the Church Militant.

The consideration of the opinion of the University of Paris

In the year one thousand four hundred XXXI, on Saturday, the XIXth day of May,

The Judges assembled in the chapel of the archiepiscopal manor of Rouen, before the Bishop of Beauvais and the Vice-lnquisitor of the Faith: Maîtres Raoul Roussel, Nicolas de Venderès, the Abbot of Fécamp, André Marguerie, Jean Pichon, Jean de Châtillon, Evrard Emengard, Guillaume Le Boucher, the Prior of Longueville, Jean Beaupère, Nicolas Midi, Maurice du Chêne, Pierre de Hodeng, Jean Lefèvre, the Abbot of Mortemer, the Prior of Saint Lô, Pierre Maurice, Jacques Quesdon, the Abbot of Cormeilles, Jean Foucher, Thomas de Courcelles, Nicolas de Couppequesne, Raoul Silvestre, Jean Pigache, Richard Gruchel, Nicolas Loiseleur, Pasquier de Vaux, Denis Gastinel, Jean Mauger, Jean Secart, Jean Adensem, Geoffroi du Crotoy, Guillaume de la Chambre, Jean du Quemyn, Martin Ladvenu, Ysambard de la Pierre, Guillaume de Lyvet, Jean Le Doulx, Jean Colombel, Richard Dessaul, Laurens du Bosc, Pierre le Mynier, Pierre Carré and Raoul Auguy.

In the presence of all of these, the Bishop of Beauvais read at length the report of the trial of Jeanne.

This done, on the advice of all the judges it was ordered that the Articles that had been sent to the University of Paris should be read in their presence.

[*After the Opinion of the University had been considered by the doctors and masters assembled at Rouen,
these latter agreed with it, and advised that it should be
read to Jeanne, and that she should be charitably admonished and warned before a final Sentence was pronounced.*]

The reading of the censures of the University
Read and pronounced by Maître Pierre Maurice, doctor
in theology, together with the University's deliberations
upon each of the Articles.

Firstly, he addressed himself to Jeanne, saying to her:

I

You, Jeanne, have said that from the age of thirteen you
have had revelations and apparitions of angels, of Saint
Catherine and of Saint Margaret, and that you have frequently seen them with your bodily eyes; and that they
have spoken to you.

On this first point the clerks of the University of Paris
have considered the form of the said revelations and
apparitions and the purpose and matter of the things
revealed, and the condition of the person. Taking all these
things into consideration, they have said and declared that
all the afore-mentioned things are lies, untrue, pernicious
and evil; and that all such revelations are superstitious,
and proceed from evil and devilish spirits.

II

You have said that your king had a sign whereby he knew
that you were sent from God; for Saint Michael, accompanied by several angels, some having wings, and others

crowns, and with them Saint Catherine and Saint Margaret, came to you in the castle of Chinon, and climbed the steps of the castle as far as the hall of your king, before whom the angel who carried a crown, bowed. On one occasion you said that when your king received this sign, he was alone; on another occasion you said that this crown, which you call 'a sign', was given to the Archbishop of Reims, who handed it to your king in the presence of several princes and lords whom you named.

As for this Article, the clerks say that it is not true; but is a presumptuous lie, seductive and pernicious, and a pretence that is derogatory of both ecclesiastical and angelic dignity.

III

You have said that you recognized the angels and the saints by the good advice, and the comfort and teaching that they gave you. And you also believe that it was Saint Michael who appeared to you; and you declare that their deeds and words are good; and that you believe this as firmly as you believe the Faith of Jesus Christ.

As for this Article, the clerks say that such things are not sufficient to [enable you to] recognize these angels and saints; that you believed too lightly and affirmed your belief too rashly; and that inasmuch as you make a comparison saying you believe these things as firmly as you believe in the Faith of Jesus Christ, you err in the faith.

IV

You have said that you are aware of certain things to come, and that you have known hidden secrets; and that you have recognized people whom you had never seen before; and that you have done so by means of the voices of Saint Catherine and Saint Margaret.

As for this Article, they say that in this matter there are both superstition and divination, presumptuous assertion, and vain boasting.

V

You have said that, by God's command, you have continually worn man's dress, wearing the short robe, doublet, and hose attached by points; that you have also worn your hair short, cut *en rond* above your ears, with nothing left that could show you to be a woman; and that on many occasions you received the Body of our Lord dressed in this fashion, although you have been frequently admonished to leave it off, which you have refused to do, saying that you would rather die than leave it off, save by God's command. And you said further that if you were still so dressed and with the king and those of his party, it would be one of the greatest blessings for the kingdom of France; and you have said that not for anything would you take an oath not to wear this dress or carry arms; and concerning all these matters you have said that you did well, and obediently to God's command.

As for these points, the clerks say that you blaspheme God in His sacraments; that you transgress divine law, the Holy Scriptures and the canon law; you hold the Faith doubtfully and wrongly; you boast vainly; you are suspect of idolatry; and you condemn yourself in being unwilling to wear the customary clothing of your sex, and following the custom of the Gentiles and the heathen.

VI

You have said that often in your letters you have put the two names JESUS MARIA and the sign of the Cross, in token that those to whom you have written should not do that which is contained in your letters; and in others of your letters you have boasted that you would see by the result who had the best right; and on many occasions you said that you had done nothing save by revelation and by God's command.

As for this Article, the clerks say that you are cruel and a murderess, desirous of the shedding of human blood, seditious, provoking to tyranny, and blaspheming God and His commandments and revelations.

VII

You have said that, following the revelations you had had, at the age of seventeen you left your father and mother against their will, causing them such anxiety that they went almost out of their minds. And you went to Robert de Baudricourt, who, at your request, gave you a man's garments and a sword, and also men to lead you to your king, to whom you said that you had come to drive out his enemies; and you promised him that you would install him in his kingdom; and that he would have victory over all his enemies; and that God had sent you to do so. And you said that you had done all these things in obedience to God's revelation.

As for this Article, the clerks say that you have acted wrongly and impetuously towards your father and mother, therein transgressing the commandment of God to honour thy father and thy mother; that you have behaved scandalously, blaspheming God and erring in the Faith. And the promise that you made to your king was presumptuous and rash.

VIII

You have said that of your own will you leaped from the tower of Beaurevoir into the moat, preferring to die rather than to be put in the hands of the English and to live on after the destruction of Compiègne; and that Saint Catherine and Saint Margaret forbade you to leap, but you could not refrain from doing so, although you sinned greatly in leaping contrary to their orders; but you have since learned from your voices that God had forgiven the sin, after you had confessed it.

As for this Article, the clerks say that in this was cowardice tending to despair and to suicide; and that you have made a rash and presumptuous assertion in saying that God had forgiven the sin; showing that you wrongly understand [the doctrine of] free-will and man's right to choose.

IX

You have said that Saint Catherine and Saint Margaret promised to bring you to heaven, provided you kept your virginity which you vowed and promised them. And of this you are as certain as if you were already in the glory of Paradise; and you do not believe that you have committed mortal sin; for if you were in mortal sin, Saint Catherine and Saint Margaret would not come to you as they do.

As for this Article, the clerks say that herein you are guilty of a rash and presumptuous assertion and of pernicious lies; that you contradict what you previously said, and that you incorrectly understand the Christian Faith.

X

You have said that you are well assured that God loves certain others living more than yourself, and that you know this by revelation from these saints, who speak in the French language; and not in English, because they are not of their party. And that, ever since you learned that the voices were on your king's side, you have not loved the Burgundians.

As for this Article, the clerks say that this is a rash presumption and assertion, blasphemy against the saints, and transgression of God's commandment to love one's neighbour.

XI

You have said that to those whom you call Saint Michael, Saint Catherine and Saint Margaret you made several reverences, kneeling and kissing the ground they walked on, and vowing your virginity to them; and even that you have kissed and embraced them, and from the beginning [believed] that they came from God, without asking advice from your curé or from any churchman; but that none the less you believe that this voice has come from God, as firmly as you believe in the Christian Faith and that Jesus Christ suffered His death and passion; and that if any evil spirits were to appear in the form and feature of Saint Michael, you would know it. You have also said that not for anyone in the world would you tell the sign given to your king, save by God's command.

To which the clerks say that, supposing you have had the revelations and apparitions of which you boast, in the way that you say, you are an idolater, and invoker of demons, a wanderer from the Faith, and have rashly taken an unlawful oath.

XII

You have said that if the Church desired you to do the opposite of the commandment which you say you have received from God, you would not do so for anything in the world. And you know for certain that what is contained in your trial came by God's command; and that it would impossible for you to do the contrary. And that, concerning all the afore-mentioned matters, you are not willing to refer them to the judgment of the Church on earth, nor of any man alive, but only to God alone. And you say further that you do not give your answers of your own intelligence, but by command of God, regardless of the fact that the article of the Faith which says that everyone must believe in the Catholic Church has been several times explained to you; and that every good Catholic Christian must submit all his deeds to the Church, and especially facts concerning revelations and such-like.

As for this Article, the clerks say that you are schismatic, having no comprehension of the truth and authority of the Church; and that up to the present you have perniciously erred in the faith of God.

The charitable admonition

After the Articles had been read to Jeanne, together with the Opinion of the University of Paris, she was admonished by the said doctor that she should carefully consider her words and deeds, especially with reference to the final Article; speaking to her as follows:

Jeanne, my very dear friend, it is now time, at the end of your trial, to think carefully of what you have said and done.

For since both by the Bishop of Beauvais, the Vice-Inquisitor, and other doctors sent to you to admonish you, both in public and in secret, for the honour of the Faith and law of Jesus Christ, for the peace of Christian people, and on account of the scandal which it causes, as well as for the salvation of your soul and of your body, you have been very carefully warned; you have also been told of the punishments which may be inflicted upon you, both in soul and body, if you do not correct and amend your words and deeds, and submit to the judgment of the Church.

Up to the present you have been unwilling to heed these warnings. And although in your own deeds and words there has been matter enough to find you guilty, yet the judges, desiring your salvation both of body and soul, sent to the University of Paris, the light of all knowledge and the extirpation of all error, in order that your words and deeds at your trial might be thoroughly examined.

In accordance with the opinion of the University, the judges ordered that you should be over and over again charitably admonished, warning you of the errors, scandals and other sins you have committed, and begging and praying for the love of Our Lord Jesus Christ, Who suffered so cruel a death to redeem mankind, that you should correct your words and deeds, and submit to the judgment of the Church, as every loyal Christian is obliged to do; and not allow yourself to be separated from Our Lord Jesus Christ, that you may be a partaker of His glory; nor choose the way of eternal damnation with the enemies of God, who are always endeavouring to molest and disturb men, sometimes counterfeiting the likeness of angels or saints, and pretending to be such, as appears in the lives of the Fathers. Therefore if such apparitions appear to you, do not believe them, but reject and cast out such follies and imaginations, in agreement with the statements and opinions of the University of Paris and the other doctors, who are conversant with and understand God's law and the Holy Scriptures; to whom it seems that one should give no credence to such apparitions and other novelties, unless they are justified in Holy Scripture or by some other sign as being miraculous. In these you have believed most lightly, without having recourse to God in devout prayer, in order that you might be made certain in the matter; nor have you had recourse to any prelate or other wise and learned churchman, who would have been able to inform you of the truth; which, considering your condition and the simplicity of your knowledge, you ought to have done.

Take for example: if your king in the exercise of his power had given you charge of a certain place, forbidding you to let anyone enter; and [some-one came], saying he came by the king's authority, you would not allow him to enter unless he brought you letters or some other certain sign that he came with the king's authority; likewise Our Lord Jesus Christ, when He ascended into heaven, leaving the government of the Church to Saint Peter and his successors, forbade them to receive any coming in His Name, if they were not sufficiently assured, other than by their own words, that they came from God.

Thus we should not have faith in your words, since God has forbidden it.

Wherefore, Jeanne, you must understand that, if in your king's realms, when you were there, a knight or some other subject had arisen and said, I will not obey the king, nor will I submit to any of his officers, would you not have said that he should be condemned? What would you say therefore of yourself, brought up in the Faith of Jesus Christ by the sacrament of baptism, and made the spouse of Jesus Christ, if you do not obey His officers, the prelates of the Church? What judgment would you pass upon yourself? Cast off, I beg you, these opinions, if you love God your Spouse and your Salvation, and be obedient to the Church and submit yourself to its judgment. And be well assured that if you do not do so, but persevere in your errors, your soul will be condemned to eternal torment in hell; and as for your body, I do not doubt that it will come to perdition.

I beg you not to allow yourself to be held back by human shame and useless fear, by which perchance you are detained, that you may lose the great honours in which you formerly lived. Put first God's honour and the salvation of your body and your soul, and remember that if you do not do what I say, but continue in your errors, you will separate yourself from the Church and the Faith which you promised [to hold] in the holy sacrament of baptism, and will despise the authority of God and the Church, which is led and governed by Our Lord; for He has said to its prelates, He that heareth you heareth Me; and he that despiseth you despiseth Me. Therefore if you

will not submit to the Church, you are unwilling to submit yourself to God, and you err in this article of faith:
We believe in the Catholic Church, whose authority has
been sufficiently explained to you in the preceding
Articles and admonitions.

Therefore, in view of these matters, on behalf of my
lord the bishop, here present, and of my lord the
Inquisitor of the Faith, your judges, I do admonish, beg
and exhort you, by the pity that you feel for the Passion of
Our Saviour your Creator, and the desire you must have
for the salvation of your soul and body, to correct and
amend your faults and return into the way of truth, obey-
ing and submitting yourself to the judgment and decision
of the Church. And in so doing you will save your soul,
and deliver, as I hope, your body from death. But if you
do the contrary, and persist [in your evil courses], be
assured that your soul will be damned, and I fear also the
destruction of your body. From which may God preserve
you. Amen.

After Jeanne had been thus admonished, and had
heard all the exhortations, she answered in the manner
following:

As for my words and deeds, I refer to what I said at my
trial, and I will maintain them.

Questioned by the said Maître Pierre [Maurice] if she
believes that she is not bound to submit her words and
deeds to the Church Militant or to any other than God,

She answered: I will maintain what I have always said
at my trial.

And if I were to be condemned and saw the fire lit and
the wood prepared and the executioner who was to burn
me ready to cast me into the fire, still in the fire would I

not say anything other than I have said. And I will maintain what I have said until death.

After this, the judges asked the promoter of the trial and Jeanne herself if either of them wished to say anything further, to which they both answered no.

Then the bishop proceeded to the conclusion of the trial, according to a schedule which he held in his hands, of which the tenor follows.

We, the judges competent in this trial, declare and have declared Ourselves so to be, as much as is required, and declare this trial ended. And We do assign to-morrow to hear Our verdict in this matter, and to proceed further in accordance with law and equity.

In the presence of Brother Ysambard de la Pierre and Messire Matthew le Basteur, [52] priests; and Louis Coursel, clerk; of the dioceses of Rouen, London and Noyon; witnesses.

[*Here in the Orléans manuscript is a statement that the writer intends to include the opinion of Jean Gerson, who believed Jeanne innocent of all the charges. For some reason unknown to us, this opinion was never included in the manuscript.*]

The abjuration
[At a solemn assembly publicly held in the cemetery of Saint Ouen at Rouen, before the lord Bishop of Beauvais and the Vice-Inquisitor, in the presence of the most reverend father in Christ Henry, Cardinal of England, the reverend fathers in Christ the lord Bishops of Thérouanne, Noyon and Norwich, together with the

lords and masters, Jean Beaupère, Nicolas Midi, Nicolas
de Venderès, André Marguerie, Denis Gastinel, Jean de
Châtillon, the lord abbots of Saint Ouen, Fécamp and
Saint Michel-au-péril-de-la-mer, Maurice du Chêne, Jean
Pinchon and Jean Alespée ... after the sermon (from the
fifteenth chapter of Saint John, 'A branch cannot bear
fruit of itself except it abide in the vine'), [53] the preacher said to Jeanne: 'Here are my lords the judges, who have
time and again summoned and required you to submit
your words and deeds to our Mother Holy Church, inasmuch as it seems to the learned clerks that there are many
things contained in these words and deeds which it is not
good either to say or to uphold.'

To which Jeanne replied: 'I will answer you.' As to submission to the Church she said, 'I have already told you
that concerning all that I have done I appeal, after God, to
our Holy Father the Pope. Everything that I have done, I
have done at God's command.' ... And she was told that
this did not suffice, for it was not possible to send to the
Holy Father, being so far away, and that the Ordinaries
were each one judge in his own diocese, and that therefore
she must submit to our Mother Holy Church. She was
thus admonished three times.

And when the Sentence was partly read, she said that
she was willing to hold all that the judges and the Church
desired, and to be obedient to them. [54]

Then, in the presence of the afore-named persons and
a great multitude of people, she recanted and made her
abjuration in the manner following.]

HERE FOLLOWS THE ABJURATION OF JEANNE THE PUCELLE,
MADE THE XXIIIIth OF MAY, IN THE YEAR MIIIIXXXI

All those who have erred and been at fault in the Christian Faith, and have since by God's grace returned into the light of truth, and into the unity of our Mother Holy Church, must take extreme care that the enemy of hell does not cause them to relapse into error and damnation.

Here follows the tenor of the schedule which the Bishop of Beauvais and the other judges said was made by the said Jeanne and signed by her hand,

The which I do not believe,

And it is not believable that she intended that which is here shown. [55]

I JEANNE, CALLED THE PUCELLE, A MISERABLE SINNER, AFTER I RECOGNIZED THE SNARE OF ERROR IN WHICH I WAS HELD; AND NOW THAT I HAVE, BY GOD'S GRACE, RETURNED TO OUR MOTHER HOLY CHURCH; IN ORDER THAT IT MAY BE APPARENT THAT NOT FEIGNEDLY BUT WITH GOOD HEART AND WILL I HAVE RETURNED TO HER; I DO CONFESS THAT I HAVE GRIEVOUSLY SINNED, IN FALSELY PRETENDING THAT I HAVE HAD REVELATIONS FROM GOD AND HIS ANGELS, SAINT CATHERINE AND SAINT MARGARET, ETC.

AND ALL MY WORDS AND DEEDS WHICH ARE CONTRARY TO THE CHURCH, I DO REVOKE; AND I DESIRE TO LIVE IN UNITY WITH THE CHURCH, NEVERMORE DEPARTING THERE-FROM.

IN WITNESS WHEREOF MY SIGN MANUAL,

signed JHENNE +

The reading of the Sentence

Here follows the Definitive Sentence, pronounced by the Bishop of Beauvais, after the abjuration and the [signing of the] schedule, beginning:

IN THE NAME OF THE LORD, AMEN

All pastors of the Church who would faithfully lead God's people, must carefully and diligently watch lest the devil, through his subtle arts, seduces and deceives the flock of Jesus Christ, to do which he labours ceaselessly. Wherefore there is need of great diligence to resist his false and sinful wiles.

Since you, Jeanne, commonly called the Pucelle, have been found guilty of many errors in the Faith of Jesus Christ, for which you have been called to judgment, and concerning which you have been heard; and since all the points and articles of your trial, your confessions, answers and assertions have been examined by Us, and the whole trial has been seen and deliberated on by the masters and doctors of the Faculty of Theology in Paris, as well as by a number of prelates and doctors in law, both canon and civil, who are in this town of Rouen, by whom you have been charitably admonished with long appeals for your change of heart.

Notwithstanding these warnings and remonstrances, and after the adjuration made to you, you have rashly and wantonly fallen into sin.

Wherefore, that you may make salutary penance, We have condemned you, and do now condemn you by this Definitive Sentence to perpetual imprisonment, [56] with the bread of sorrow and the water of affliction, that you may weep for your sins, and nevermore commit them.

Saving Our grace and moderation, if hereafter you shall deserve them.

[*Here, and out of chronological order, Orléans inserts an incorrect version of the scene at St Ouen. This I have replaced above by the correct version taken from d'Urfé.*]

Visit of the Inquisitor to the prison

After the Sentence was pronounced, as has been said, the Vice-Inquisitor and several others who had been present at the Sentence, went to see Jeanne after dinner in the prison in which she was kept. They remonstrated with her, pointing out that the Church had dealt kindly with her, and that she should accept the Sentence with humility and be obedient to the Church; that she should leave her revelations and other stupidities; warning her that if she should again fall into such sins, the Church would not take her back; and begging her to leave off man's clothes and wear a woman's dress.

To this Jeanne replied that she would willingly wear woman's dress and be obedient to the Church.

And immediately she put on a woman's dress, and allowed her hair. which had been cut *en rond*, to be cut off. [57]

The Trial for Relapse

Visit of the judges to the prison
The following Monday, the twenty-eighth day of May, the judges went to the prison, and found [Jeanne] dressed in man's clothing, that is, a robe, hood, and the other garments normally worn by men, which garments she had left off by order of the Church.

Asked for what reason she had again taken man's dress,

She answered that she had done so just now.

Asked why, and who had induced her to do so,

She said, of her own will. And that nobody had forced her to do so. And that she preferred man's dress to woman's.

Wherefore she was reminded that she had sworn and promised never again to wear male clothing,

To which she replied that she had never intended to take an oath not to take man's dress again.

Being asked several times why she had taken it again,

She said that she had done so because it seemed to her more suitable and convenient to wear man's dress being with men, than to wear a woman's dress.

She said further that she had again taken it because they had not kept their promise that she should hear Mass; that she should receive the Body of the Lord; and that she should be relieved of her fetters.

And that she would rather die than be kept in irons.

But if they promised that she should go to Mass and have her fetters removed, she would do everything the Church ordered and required.

Questioned whether since last Thursday she had heard the voices of Saint Catherine and Saint Margaret,

She answered yes.

And that they told her that God had sent her word by them that she had put herself in great danger of perdition in that she had consented to make the abjuration and renunciation in order to save her life; and that she was damned for doing so.

And she said that, before Thursday, her voices had told her what she ought to do, and that she had done it.

She said also that her voices had told her that, when she was on the platform, she should answer the preacher boldly. And she said that the preacher was a false preacher, for he said that she had done many things which she had never done.

She said further that in saying that God had not sent her she had damned herself, for truly God had sent her. And since Thursday her voices had told her that she had done great wrong to God in confessing that what she had done was not well done.

She said also that everything she had said and revoked, she had done only through fear of the fire.

Asked if she believes that the voices are those of Saint Catherine and Saint Margaret,

She answered yes; and that they came from God.

Asked to tell the truth about the afore-mentioned crown,

She answered that she had told the truth in everything, as best she could.

It was then said to her that when she was on the platform before the judges and the people, when she made her abjuration, she had been adjured to tell the truth. And you admitted [they said], that you had boasted falsely that the voices you said you heard were those of Saint Catherine and Saint Margaret.

To which she answered that she never intended to have denied her apparitions, that is, that they were Saint Catherine and Saint Margaret. And what she said, she said for fear of the fire. And if she recanted, it was untrue.

She also said that she would rather do penance by dying, than bear any longer the agony of imprisonment.

And she said that never had she done anything contrary to God and the Faith, anything that they had made her revoke; and as for what was contained in the schedule of abjuration, she never intended it.

And she never intended to revoke anything, unless it was pleasing to God that she should do so.

She said further, if the judges desire it, she will wear a woman's dress again. For the rest, she knows no more.

Decision of the judges to hand over Jeanne to the secular arm

On Tuesday the twenty-ninth day of May, We, the Bishop of Beauvais, called together the doctors and other ecclesiastics in great number in the chapel of the Archiepiscopal Manor, and explained to them that Jeanne had been again and again admonished to return into the way of truth. And how, after being so admonished before the people, she had sworn that never would she relapse, and had signed a schedule with her own hand; and on Thursday after dinner, being the day of her Sentence, she had been charitably admonished by the Vice-Inquisitor and others that she should continue in her good intentions and take great care she did not relapse.

But, being persuaded by the devil, she had declared time and again, in the presence of several persons, that her voices, who had been accustomed to appear to her, had come again; and she had taken off her woman's dress and again taken man's clothing.

And after this, before all the clerks who were present in the chapel, the confessions and assertions which she had made the day before were read; after which, their opinions were asked as to what should be done, and they were all of the opinion and stated that she ought to be considered a heretic, and should be left to secular justice, with a request that they should treat her more kindly than she had deserved.

[*At seven the next morning Jeanne was visited in her cell by the two Dominicans, Ladvenu and Toutmouillé, who came to prepare her for death. The former heard her in confession, and (most inconsistently in the case of a judgment for relapse) Cauchon permitted her to receive Holy Communion.*

It is impossible to understand what Cauchon meant when he gave this permission; the reception of the Sacrament by a relapsed person, necessarily unabsolved, is not consonant with the fact that communion demands the pre-requisite of absolution. If she were absolved, she could no longer be in lapse.

The Host was brought to her cell, as Massieu said, 'irreverently, without stole and lights, at which Brother

Martin, who had confessed her, was ill-content, and so a stole and lights were sent for, and thus Brother Martin administered It to her. It is on record that Jeanne said to her confessor, 'Where shall I be to-night?' to which he replied, 'Have you no faith in Our Lord?' 'Yes, God help-ing me, to-day I shall be with Him in Paradise.']

The Definitive Sentence

And on Wednesday the penultimate day of May, being the last day of the trial,

By Us the said Jeanne was cited to hear the law and to appear in person before Us in the Old Market of the town of Rouen at eight o'clock in the morning, to see herself declared relapsed into her errors, heretic and excommuni-cate; together with the intimations customary to be made in such a case.

Later on the same day, at about nine o'clock in the morning, We the bishop and judges being in the Old Market of Rouen, near to the church of Saint Sauveur, in the presence of the Bishops of Thérouanne and Noyon, and several other doctors, clerks and masters, after the sermon had been preached, We admonished Jeanne, for the salvation of her soul, that she should repent her evil deeds and show true contrition, by means of counsel from two Friar Preachers, who were near her in order that they might continually advise her, whom for this purpose We had appointed.

All these matters referred to being done, We, the afore-said bishop and Vice-Inquisitor, having regard to the afore-mentioned matters wherein it appeared that Jeanne remained obstinate in her errors, and through malice and devilish obstinacy held falsely shown signs of contrition and penitence; and that she had blasphemed the holy and divine Name of God; and showing herself an incorrigible heretic had relapsed into heresy and error, and was unworthy and incapable of any pity,

We proceeded to the Definitive Sentence in the manner following:

IN THE NAME OF THE LORD, AMEN

We Pierre, by Divine pity, humble Bishop of Beauvais, and We, Brother Jean le Maître, deputy of the Inquisitor of the Faith, judges competent in this matter,

Since you, Jeanne, called the Pucelle, have been found by Us relapsed into divers errors and crimes of schism, idolatry, invocation of devils, and various other wickednesses,

And since for these reasons by just judgment We have found you so to be,

Nevertheless, since the Church never closes her arms to those who would return to her, We did believe that, with full understanding and unfeigned faith, you had left all the errors which you had renounced, vowing, swearing and publicly promising that never again would you fall into such errors, nor into any other heresies, but would live in Catholic unity and communion with our Church and our Holy Father the Pope, as is stated in a schedule signed by your own hand.

None the less time and again you have relapsed, as a dog that returns to its vomit, as We do state with great sorrow.

Wherefore We declare that you have again incurred the Sentence of excommunication which you formerly incurred, and are again fallen into your previous errors, for which reasons We now declare you to be a heretic.

And by this Sentence, seated upon Our tribunal of justice, as it is herein written, We do cast you forth and reject you from the communion of the Church as an infected limb, and hand you over to secular justice, praying the same to treat you with kindness and humanity in respect of your life and of your limbs. [58]

The execution

After the Sentence was read, the bishop, the Inquisitor, and many of the judges went away, leaving Jeanne upon the scaffold.

Then the Bailli of Rouen, an Englishman, who was there, without any legal formality and without reading any Sentence against her, ordered that she should be taken to the place where she was to be burned.

When Jeanne heard this order given, she began to weep and lament in such a way that all the people present were themselves moved to tears.

The said Bailli immediately ordered that the fire should be lighted, which was done.

And she was there burned and martyred tragically, an act of unparalleled cruelty.

And many, both noble and peasant, murmured greatly against the English.

Notes

Introduction

[1]   Cf. the subtitle from V. Sackville-West, *Saint Joan of Arc: burned as a heretic, May 30, 1431, canonised as a saint, May 16, 1920* (London, 1973 [1st edn, 1936]).

[2]   Marina Warner, *Joan of Arc: the image of female heroism* (London, 1981). The film: *Joan of Arc*, prod. by Jeremy Newson and dir. by Gina Newson. A Tattooist International Production for Channel Four, Channel Four Productions Ltd., 1983.

[3]   Jeffrey Burton Russell clearly states: 'The trial of Saint Joan deserves no place of importance in the history of the witch phenomenon', *Witchcraft in the Middle Ages* (Ithaca and London, 1972), p. 262; cf. also Richard Kieckhefer, *European Witch Trials: their foundations in popular and learned culture, 1300–1500* (London, 1976), about Joan: pp. 23, 123, 171 note 86.

[4]   Warner, *Joan of Arc*, pp. 247–8: 'the later traveller'; Edmond Richer, *Histoire de la Pucelle d'Orléans*, texte collationné et publié ... par Philippe-Hector Dunand. La première histoire en date de Jeanne d'Arc (1625–1630) (Paris, 1911, 2 vols.) I, p. 67.

[5]   Marina Warner, *Alone of All Her Sex: the myth and the cult of the Virgin Mary* (London, 1976), pp. 281–3.

[6]   Robert Graves, *The White Godess: an historical grammar of poetic myth* (London, 1977 [1st edn 1961]), pp. 175–6.

[7]   Cf. Keith Thomas, *Religion and the Decline of Magic: studies in popular beliefs in sixteenth- and seventeenth-century England* (Harmondsworth, 1984 [1st edn 1971]), pp. 724 ff.

[8]   Cf. Marina Warner, *The Absent Mother, or women against women in the 'old wives' tale'* (Hilversum, 1991), p. 24.

[9]   Carlo Ginzburg, *Ecstasies: deciphering the witches' sabbath*, trans. Raymond Rosenthal, ed. Gregory Elliott (London etc., 1990), pp. 105–6, 185.

[10] Cf. Russell, *Witchcraft*, pp. 273–5.

[11] Warner, *Absent Mother*, pp. 26 ff; see also Marina Warner, *From*

The Trial of Joan of Arc

the Beast to the Blonde: on fairy tales and their tellers (London, 1994), *passim*.

[12] Cf. R. K. Davis, *Peleus and Thetis* (London, 1924).

[13] Cf. Bruno Bettelheim, *The Uses of Enchantment* (Harmondsworth: Penguin, 1978).

[14] Sackville-West, *Saint Joan of Arc*, 39: 'All these stories, however silly and childish, were a part of rustic life'; cf. Tisset-Lanhers, *Procès* II, 65–8; 87; Scott, *Trial*, 75-6; 87-8; cf. Pernoud, *Retrial*, 62–5.

[15] Pernoud, *Retrial*, 56: Fontaine aux Rains; note 3: Fontaine des Groselliers.

[16] Cf. Norman Cohn, *Europe's Inner Demons: an enquiry inspired by the great witch-hunt* (New York, 1975), 213.

[17] Scott, *Trial*, 75–6; quotation: p. 75 (cf. Tisset-Lanhers, *Procès* II, pp. 65–8).

[18] Scott, *Trial*, p. 86: Asked whether Saint Catherine and Saint Margaret had spoken to her beneath the tree, she answered: I do not know. Being repeatedly asked if the saints had spoken to her at the aforementioned spring, she replied Yes; and she had heard them there (cf. Tisset-Lanhers, *Procès* II, p. 85).

[19] Warner, *Joan of Arc*, p. 250: Lionel Royer's frescoes at Domrémy; ill. 43, in front of p. 229: the *tableau-vivant*.

[20] Tisset-Lanhers, *Procès* II, p. 99.

[21] Scott, *Trial*, pp. 96–7; Tisset-Lanhers, *Procès* II, pp. 99–100.

[22] Warner, *Joan of Arc*, pp. 80–81; cf. Scott, *Trial*, pp. 101–2; Tisset-Lanhers, *Procès* II, pp. 107–8.

[23] Warner, *Joan of Arc*, p. 124; Scott, *Trial*, pp. 77–8; Tisset-Lanhers, *Procès* II, p. 71.

[24] Warner, *Joan of Arc*, pp. 120, 177–8; cf. Pernoud, *Retrial*, p. 106. Saint Louis is still considered a saint, but Charlemagne has dropped out of the liturgical calendar.

[25] Murray, *Witch-cult*.

[26] Cohn, *Europe's Inner Demons*, p. 107 ff.

[27] See note 9; cf. Carlo Ginzburg, 'Deciphering the Sabbath', in Bengt Ankarloo and Gustav Henningsen, *Early Modern European Witchcraft: centres and peripheries* (Oxford, 1990), pp. 121–37 ('a summary, provisional in some respects, of the conclusion of ... Ginzburg, *Storia Notturna: una decifrazione del sabba*, Torino, 1989)'.

[28] Warner, *Joan of Arc*, p. 98. For this question: Anneliese Maier, 'Eine Verfügung Johanns XXII über die Zuständigkeit de

Inquisition für Zaubereiprozesse' in: Maier, *Augeshendes Mittelalter. Gesammelte Aufsätze zur Geistesgeschichte des 14, Jahrhunderts* II: *Storia e letteratura*. Raccolata di studi e testi 65 (Roma, 1967), pp. 59–80 [=*Archivum Fratrum Praedicatorum* XXII (1952), 226–46] (*c.* 1320); cf. Russell, *Witchcraft*, pp. 173–4; 204: '...any invocation of demons was justly within the limits of Inquisitorial jurisdiction' (Pope Gregory XI in 1374).

[29] 'What did popular report say of that tree which is called the "Ladies' Tree"? Were girls in the habit of gathering there to dance? And what of this fountain that is near the tree? Did Joan go there with other girls, and for what reasons and when did she go?', Pernoud, *Retrial*, p. 225; Appendix III: 'The interrogatory taken in Lorraine', IX.

[30] *Ibid.*, p. 58.

[31] '*Faciunt hominem de Maio*', Ayroles, *La vraye Jeanne d'Arc* II, p. 205: Colin, son of Jean Colin from Greux, aged 50.

[32] Jack-in-the-green: a boy dressed as a chimney sweep, enclosed in a leaf-covered wicker frame in May Day sports (*Webster's Dictionary*).

[33] Kieckhefer, *Witch Trials, p.* 44; cf. Russell, *Witchcraft*, ch. 9: 'The classical formulation of of the witch phenomenon 1427–1486'.

[34] Warner, *Joan of Arc*, pp. 97–8; Vale, *Charles VII*, 29.

[35] Gilles de Rais: Russsell, *Witchcraft, pp.* 262–3; D'Alençon: Vale, *Charles VII*, pp. 155–62; 204–9; Pernoud-Clin, *Jeanne d'Arc*, pp. 276–8.

[36] Shakespeare, *Henry VI, Part* 2, Act II, Scene 3: Margery Jourdain, 'the witch in Smithfield', was to be burned, Eleanore's three associates were to be strangled on the gallows; 'You madam, for you are more noble born, / Despoiled of your honour in your life, / Shall, / after three days' open penance done, / Live in your country here, in banishment, / With Sir John Stanley, in the Isle of Man'; the 'open penance': Scene IV: 'Uneath may she endure the flinty streets, / To tread them with her tender-feeling feet.' etc.; Kieckhefer, *Witch Trials*, p. 126 (with references), cf. V. J. Scattergood, *Politics and Poetry in the Fifteenth Century* (London, 1971), pp. 146–7: Eleanore as mermaid and witch in a poem of 1428 (*Complaint of my Lady of Gloucester*, possibly written by John Lydgate); pp. 152–5: Eleanore's vicissitudes were dealt with immediately in the poem *Lament of the Duchess of Gloucester*, cf. E. F. Jacob, *The Fifteenth Century, 1399–1485*, The Oxford History of England

The Trial of Joan of Arc

VI (Oxford, 1969), pp. 485–6: reference to a poem *Compleint against fortune*, possibly written by Sir Richard Roos.

[37] Ayroles, *La vraye Jeanne d'Arc* IV, p. 285, also cited in the *Malleus maleficarum* (The hammer of the witches), written in 1486: Alan C. Kors and Edward Peters (eds.), *Witchcraft in Europe, 1100–1700: a documentary history* (Philadelphia, 1972), pp. 115–16 (quotation from *Malleus maleficarum*, trans. Montague Summers, London, 1968); cf. the best modern translation, Jakob Sprenger / Heinrich Institoris, *Der Hexenhammer (Malleus maleficarum)*, aus dem Lateinischen übertragen und einegeleitet von J. W. R. Schmidt (München, 1985 [1st edn: Berlin, 1906]), pp. 93–4.

[38] Saul at Endor: 1 Samuel 28.7–25; cf. *Malleus maleficarum* (ed. Schmidt), I, p. 197. The picture: RM A 668.

[39] Cohn, *Europe's Inner Demons*, pp. 100 (the mark; cf. Murray, *Witch-cult*, pp. 86–96), 226, 228–30; cf Russell, *Witchcraft*, pp. 219–20. See, for example, *La Vauderye de Lyonois en brief*, in Joseph Hansen (ed.), *Quellen und Untersuchungen zur Geschichte des Hexenwahns und der Hexenverfolgung im Mittlealter* (Bonn, 1901), p. 193.

[40] Baby: Warner, *Joan of Arc*, p. 90; Tisset-Lanhers, *Procès* II, p. 98; Scott, *Trial*, p. 96; butterflies: Warner, *Joan of Arc*, p. 90; Tisset-Lanhers, *Procès* II, p. 97 (cf. art. II, *ibid.*, p. 161); Scott, *Trial*, p. 95 (cf. p. 132); Sainte Catherine de Fierbois: Warner, *Joan of Arc*, pp. 89, 91, 163–5; Tisset-Lanhers, *Procès* II, pp. 75–7; Scott, *Trial*, pp. 80–82 (cf. art XIX and XXXIII, *ibid.*, pp. 136, 138); lost cup, unworthy priest: Warner, *Joan of Arc*, p. 90; Tisset-Lanhers, *Procès* II, p. 123; Scott, *Trial*, p. 110; mandrake root: Warner, *Joan of Arc*, p. 112; Tisset-Lanhers, *Procès* II, p. 87 (cf. art VII, *ibid.*, p. 166); Scott, *Trial*, pp. 87–8 (cf. p. 133); denial of any charm: Warner, *Joan of Arc*, p. 112; Tisset-Lanhers, *Procès* II, p. 94; Scott, *Trial*, p. 93.

[41] 'a disciple and limb of the fiend (the devil)', Ayroles, *La vraye Jeanne d'Arc* III, p. 643: Pièce justificative N, cf. pp. 562–3; Warner, *Joan of Arc*, pp. 110–11.

[42] Warner, *Joan of Arc*, p. 111; Tisset-Lanhers, *Procès* II, p. 95; Scott, *Trial*, p. 93.

[43] Scott, *Trial*, p. 128, cf. p. 133: Art. V; Tisset-Lanhers, *Procès* I, p. 178, cited by Ginzburg, *Ecstasies*, p. 97; cf. Warner, *Joan of Arc*, p. 128.

[44] Warner, *Joan of Arc*, p. 96; Tisset-Lanhers, *Procès* II, p. 313.

[45] Warner, *Joan of Arc*, pp. 126–7; Kieckhefer, *Witch Trials*, p. 117; Cohn, *Europe's inner demons*, pp. 196–7; Russell, *Witchcraft*, pp. 214–15.

[46] Scott, *Trial*, pp. 152–3: 'The XIIth day of May ... the judges [13 at that moment, 12 answers] ... were asked ... whether it were expedient to put Jeanne to the torture'; one of them answered 'no' to the question 'in order that the trial ... could not be calumniated'; another simply answered that Jeanne ought not to be put to the torture and two others said 'in no circumstances'; six thought it 'not expedient to put her to torture'; according to Courcelles (who said in his deposition at the Trial of Rehabilitation that he never gave an opinion as to her being put to the torture) and Loiseleur that Jeanne ought to be put to the torture; Vice-Inquisitor Jean le Maître concluded that Jeanne 'should be questioned frequently to know if she would be willing to submit to the Church Militant'.

[47] Warner, *Joan of Arc*, p. 109; Shakespeare, *Henry VI, Part 2*, Act V, Scene 3, lines 13–15.

[48] Cf. Warner, *Joan of Arc*, pp. 23–4; 235–6; cf. pp. 103, 106–8: contrasted to harlotry.

[49] P. Brown, *Sorcery, Demons and the Rise of Christianity*. ASA Monographs 9 (1970), pp. 21–2, cited in Warner, *Joan of Arc*, p. 295 n. 3, also published in P. R. L. Brown, *Religion and Society in the Age of St Augustine* (London, 1972), p. 119 ff.

[50] Cf. Warner, *Joan of Arc*, pp. 152–3: claims to rank and status; rejection of parental authority and male domination; p. 155: Joan's life as a 'homage to the male sphere of action', 'upward mobility', cf. p. 160: 'Joan is the personification of mobility': cf. Caroline Walker Bynum, *Holy Feast and Holy Fast: the religious significance of food to medieval women* (Berkeley, etc., 1987), pp. 287–91: some critical remarks about the significance of cross-dressing.

[51] Cf. Gábor Klaniczay's remark: 'To give just one example: the emergence of female saints in the later Middle Ages, their special access to sacred files, their prophecies, their eminent political roles, produced such anxiety in the male world that their saintly position became ambiguous. Some eminent representatives of this type, such as Joan of Arc, were on the margin between the categories of the saint and the witch. And this emergence of 'women on top' from the religious point of view definitely contributed to a renewed diabolization of the female sex in the

same period.' Gábor Klaniczay, 'Hungary: the accusations and the universe of popular magic', in Bengt Ankarloo and Gustav Henningsen (eds.), *Early Modern European Witchcraft: centres and peripheries* (Oxford, 1990), pp. 219–55, quotation: p. 241.

[52] Christine de Pisan, *Ditié de Jehanne d'Arc*, ed. A. J. Kennedy and Kenneth Varty (Oxford, 1977).

[53] Warner, *Joan of Arc*, p. 206; cf. Beatrice Gottlieb, 'The problem of feminism in the fifteenth century' in Julius Kirshner and Suzanne F. Wemple (eds.), *Women in the Medieval World: essays in honour of John F. Mundy* (Oxford, 1985), p. 355: 'Though her works do not especially sparkle with wit, there is an amused irony in her triumphant display of the ways in which God evidently approved of women much more than his creature, man, did. The best example of this is her poem on Joan of Arc ... The example of Joan was an encouragement to religious and patriotic fervour, not to acceptance of women's aptitude for the military arts.'

[54] Warner, *Joan of Arc*, pp. 233–4: Louis de Coutes, Jean D'Alençon; Pernoud, *Retrial*, pp. 138, 123.

[55] Warner, *Joan of Arc*, pp. 233–4; cf. xiii: description of ill. 28 and 29, following p. 228.

[56] Warner, *Joan of Arc*, p. 172 (defence), cf. pp. 220; 233 (Judith).

[57] Cf. *ibid.*, pp. 145–6.

[58] *Ibid.*, p. 165.

[59] Deut. 22.5; 1 Cor. 11.14–15.

[60] Warner, *Joan of Arc*, pp. 143; cf. pp. 146–7: Jean Gerson, Jacques Gélu, Henry of Gorinchem, about them: Van Herwaarden, 'Raadsel', pp. 328–32 and nn. 28–46.

[61] Warner, *Joan of Arc*, p. 145; cf. Scott, *Trial*, pp. 68, 79–80, 91–2, 106, 122–3, 134–5.

[62] Warner, *Joan of Arc*, p. 143; cf. Scott, *Trial*, p. 156: art. v (out of xii) from the censures of the University of Paris, Tisset-Lanhers, *Procès*, ii, p. 249.

[63] Cf. Warner, *Joan of Arc*, pp. 148–9.

[64] *Ibid.*, pp. 198–217: 'Amazon'.

[65] *Ibid.*, pp. 263–4. Oddly enough, the movement towards her sanctification could be illustrated by looking at the history of women wearing trousers – with which it coincides – but this is not the place to do this.

[66] Pernoud, *Retrial*, pp. 182–3.

[67] Warner, *Joan of Arc*, p. 196, cf. ill. 8, following p. 100.

[68] *Ibid.*, pp. 181–2, cf. ill. 34, following p. 228.

[69] *Ibid.*, p. 262, cf. ill. 42, following p. 228.

[70] For instance Maurice Boutet de Monvel, *Joan of Arc*, introduction by Gerald Gottleib (London, etc., 1981).

[71] Cf. Warner, *Joan of Arc*, p. 257.

[72] Cf. Anne Llewellyn Barstow, *Joan of Arc: heretic, mystic, shaman* (Lewiston NY, 1986), pp. 9–10: use and explanation of the term 'shaman'; esp. pp. 45–79: 'Charismatic heroes: Joan as shaman'; cf. pp. 124–5: Joan 'fitting herself so expertly into the role of shaman for the Armagnac French'.

[73] Warner, *Joan of Arc*, p. 260 ff.

[74] *Ibid.*, pp. 256, 260–61. For a short but thorough survey: D. W. Brogan, *The development of modern France* I: *From the fall of the empire to the Dreyfus affair* (New York, 1966), pp. 329–87: 'The Affair, *Gesta Dei per Francos*'; cf. Michel Winock, *Nationalisme, antisémitisme et fascisme en France* (Paris, 1982), pp. 145–6: '*Jeanne d'Arc et les juifs*'. '*L'Affaire*' and Anatole France's *Vie de Jeanne d'Arc*: William Searle, *The Saint and the Skeptics: Joan of Arc in the work of Mark Twain, Anatole France and Bernard Shaw* (Detroit, 1976), pp. 63–4; 86-7, cf. more generally: Carter Jefferson, *Anatole France: the politics of skepticism* (New Brunswick, 1965), ch. 4.

Text

[1] It is known from the evidence of the Inquisitor's clerk that the interrogations were in French, and only the accounts of the sittings of the court in Latin.

[2] France here refers to the parts of the country owing allegiance to Charles II.

[3] The officer in command of the guard was John Gray, a gentleman in the Household of the Duke of Bedford, who was afterwards knighted. He was assisted by John Berwoit and William Talbot. Four soldiers were engaged in the actual work of surveillance, Nicholas Bertin, Julian Flocquet, William Mouton, and another whose name is not known.

[4] In fact the *Chambre du Parement*, a smaller room off the Great Hall.

[5] The widow of one Jean Waldaires. She was nicknamed La Rousse on account of her red hair.

[6] Women were allowed to stay in the guest-house of the monastery,

which stood beside the great gateway. This gateway is the only portion of the original buildings to remain standing.

[7] *Interroguée si c'est un angèle de Dieu, sans moyen.* Courcelles writes: *Sit unus angelus, vel utrum sit a Deo, immediate.*

[8] The *beau mai* was a branch from a beech tree, traditionally used for decoration.

[9] The family of de Bourlémont were seigneurs of Domrémy. The chateau of Bourlemont still stands not far from the village.

[10] This refers to a prophesy attributed to Merlin, current in the countryside. It was to the effect that a marvellous Maid should come from the *Nemus Canutum* (*bois chesnu*) for the healing of nations.

[11] The Orléans manuscript puts the fourth and fifth sessions into one, by reason of its omission of a long passage of interrogation [here supplied from d'Estivet]. This Sunday was the second Sunday in Lent.

[12] This probably refers to the armourer from Tours who made Jeanne's armour, Colin de Montbazon.

[13] Martin V was then Pope; there were also two anti-Popes. Armagnac was a supporter of one of these, for which he had been excommunicated by Pope Martin.

[14] The whole of this passage, being taken from d'Estivet, was originally in Latin.

[15] A mandrake (*mandragora officinarum*) is a plant of the potato family. Little images made of this root, which often looked like the lower limbs of a man, were cherished as oracles, and used in witchcraft and enchantments. The mandrake was believed to shriek when torn out of the earth.

[16] A pair of scales is the emblem of the Archangel.

[17] The ecclesiastics of the Armagnac party who examined Jeanne at Poitiers.

[18] Jean de Pressy was *Receveur général des Finances* and Treasurer to the Duke of Burgundy, Phillipe le Bon, and was probably charged with the removal of Jeanne from Beaulieu to Beaurevoir.

[19] This is a mistake in the manuscript. It should read 'around an altar or a church'.

[20] Brother Richard was a preaching friar who had caught the public imagination by prophesying the end of the world for 1430.

[21] This refers to the customary belief that witches had the power of flying through air on a broomstick.

[22] These questions were designed to entrap Jeanne into making

admissions which could afterwards be brought forward as proofs of sorcery. Insects were often believed to serve as witches' familiars.

[23] In accordance with tradition, gifts of gloves were made to the knights and nobles who were present at the coronation. One of them lost his gift, and it was suggested that Jeanne used witchcraft to find them for him.

[24] See Jeanne's answers to the interrogations during the Twelfth Session, on the subject of the hackney (p. 111).

[25] The spot where Jeanne was captured is near the end of the present bridge at Compiègne, not from the railway station.

[26] Arms were in fact granted to Jeanne. They are: azure, between two fleurs-de-lis or, a royal crown of the second, supported by a sword argent fleurdelisé and pommelled of the second. The grant may be seen in the Bibliothèque Nationale (MS Fr. 5524), and the translation reads: 'The second of June 1429 the said Lord King, knowing the prowess of Jeanne the Pucelle and the victories which came of God's gift and counsel, being in the town of Chinon, granted arms to the said Jeanne for her standard and for herself, according to the ensuing pattern, giving to the Duke of Alençon and to Jeanne charge of the siege of Jargeau.'

[27] While Jeanne and her family were in Neufchâteau, she was cited to appear in the Ecclesiastical Court of Toul to answer a charge of breach of promise brought by a young man whose name remains unknown. No records of this action have been found, and our knowledge of it depends solely upon the mention of it made during her trial. It seems probable, however, that her parents had in some way arranged for her wedding with a local youth – an arrangement which Jeanne, having already made a vow to remain unmarried until her mission was accomplished, was unable to implement. However it may have been, she returned to Neufchâteau free from all further pressure to marry, and when the danger at Domrémy (which had been the cause of their flight to Neufchâteau) was past, the d'Arc family, together with their friends and neighbours, returned to their own village. At her trial it was suggested that the young man in question refused to marry Jeanne on account of her evil life and association with prostitutes at Neufchâteau.

[28] Then a prisoner of war in the Tower of London, awaiting ransom.

[29] Both Orléans and d'Urfé give this reading, but d'Estivet and

Courcelles give the reverse, that is that 'many who saw the angel would not have seen him'. Common sense would suggest that the latter version is correct.

[30] This should be Alençon: the Bastard of Orléans was not there at the time, being present at the siege of Orléans.

[31] Nothing else is known of these matters, but the suggestion of the Court was obviously that Jeanne had used sorcery in the finding of lost articles.

[32] Paris at this time was defended by two moats outside the walls, one dry and the other filled with water. Jeanne was wounded while standing on the *dos d'âne* between the wet and dry moats, outside and a little to the north of the Porte Saint Honoré, probing the depth of water with a lance.

[33] There are two feasts of Saint Martin; 4 July and 11 November.

[34] Courcelles here adds an important point: 'Jeanne first answered, concerning the immediately preceding article relative to the certainty she felt of her salvation on which she had been examined in the morning, that she meant to reply in this way provided she kept the vow ...'

[35] *Bon gré Dieu*; God being willing. The suggestion was that she had said *Bon gré mal gré*; Whether God will it or no; which was a current expression, like the English 'willy-nilly'.

[36] The château of Beaulieu was octagonal in shape, with a tower at each angle. In the centre was the keep, 50 feet in height. Guards were posted outside Jeanne's room, but otherwise she was left to herself. She was served by her own squire, d'Aulon, who had been taken prisoner with her. In the middle of the night (presumably that of June 4–5), having noticed that the planks of the floor of her room were badly fitting, Jeanne managed to remove sufficient of the flooring to let herself down to the room beneath, whence she gained the main entrance of the castle. Beside the great door was a small room, used by the sentries on duty. The key was in the lock on the outside, and it was while endeavouring to turn it and thus imprison the sentries inside, that she was seen by the night patrol, who came in at the critical moment and gave the alarm.

[37] Jeanne here refers to the minutes of the previous proceedings.

[38] See Jeanne's reply on 24 February (p. 56).

[39] *Blanc harnoys* is armour without either gilding or blazoning.

[40] This refers to the murder of the Duke of Burgundy at Montereau in 1419, in revenge for the murder by Burgundy of Louis of

Orléans in 1407. As a result of the second murder, the new duke, Philippe le Bon, took an oath that his father's assassin should never receive the crown of France.

[41] This presumably means to the Church Universal as represented by the Pope. The words *à l'Église* do not occur in either d'Urfé or d'Estivet.

[42] A ring attributed to Jeanne d'Arc (though possibly only one of several copies which were made at the time) is still extant. It is of silver, once gilt, and of primitive workmanship, with a squared bezel engraved with the letters MAR along one side, and IHS on the other. On one shoulder is the letter M and on the other a cross.

[43] The ring referred to above was a thumb ring. The custom of wearing a ring on the thumb was very usual until the early years of the sixteenth century.

[44] D'Estivet gives: *Respondit quod melius decet ipsas amplexari per inferius quam per superius.* D'Urfé gives: *Il affiert mieulx a les accoler par le bas que par hault.* This presumably means that it is more fitting to embrace the feet than the body but it seems probable that Orléans gives the more correct reading.

[45] This signifies the saying or singing of a litany.

[46] In fact a fortnight later, 2 May.

[47] This should read: Archdeacon.

[48] D'Urfé also gives *chevaliers*, but in Courcelles the word used is *clericorum.*

[49] Jeanne was shown the instruments of torture and was told that if she did not answer truthfully she would be put to the torture, in order to procure the salvation of her soul. Many years afterwards, the Master Executioner said: 'On this occasion she answered with such prudence that all present marvelled. I retired without doing anything.'

[50] The Feast of the Invention of the Cross is 3 May. In 1431 it fell on a Thursday, the day after the Public Admonition was made to Jeanne.

[51] In his deposition at the Trial of Rehabilitation, Courcelles said: 'I never gave an opinion as to her being put to the torture.'

[52] Presumably Mathew Shepherd, an English priest.

[53] In his sermon the preacher Erard grossly insulted the king, at which she could not keep silence, but called out, 'Speak of me, not of the king.' Pointing at her, he repeated 'Your king, since he listened to you, is heretic and schismatic.' Despite the imminent danger in which she stood Jeanne could not refrain from

answering, saying, 'I dare swear that my king is the most noble Christian of all Christians!' Marvellous fidelity to a worthless sovereign, who had left her succourless to die!

[54] While the sentence was being read, Loiseleur, one of the assessors, and Massieu the usher, together with Erard, began to urge Jeanne to submit rather than be burnt. Jeanne, worn out with the long strain, and but half understanding what was being said, conscious only of the imminence of the fire, at last gave in.

[55] An allusion to Jeanne's later retraction.

[56] There is a doubt as to the especial meaning attached to the words *carcer perpetuas*. The Revd Father Thurston, s.j., in *Studies* for September 1924, writes: '"Lifelong prison" ... is, undoubtedly, the natural and obvious translation; but the phrase, I submit, is shown by sundry Inquisition records to mean simply a permanent prison as opposed to the makeshift buildings which were casually employed for the purpose.' This translator thinks, however, that the usual meaning of *perpetuas*, 'perpetual' or 'lifelong', is more likely to be correct.

[57] Jeanne's hair had grown during her imprisonment. After the Abjuration, it was shaved off completely.

[58] This was a sheer formality, and never meant to be acted upon.